The Crime Buff's Guide to Outlaw Washington, DC

Ron Franscell

Guilford, Connecticut

To Mom and Dad

All photos by Ron Franscell or in the public domain unless otherwise noted.

Text design: Sheryl P. Kober
Layout: Maggie Peterson
Project editor: Meredith Dias
Maps by Alena Joy Pearce © Morris Book Publishing, LLC

Library of Congress Cataloging-in-Publication Data

Franscell, Ron, 1957–
 The crime buff's guide to outlaw Washington, DC / Ron Franscell.
  p. cm.
 Includes index.
 ISBN 978-0-7627-7385-5
1. Crime—Washington (D.C.)—History. 2. Crime—Washington Metropolitan Area—History. 3. Outlaws—Washington Metropolitan Area—Biography. 4. Criminals—Washington Metropolitan Area—Biography. 5. Historic sites—Washington Metropolitan Area—Guidebooks. 6. Washington Metropolitan Area—Guidebooks. I. Title. II. Title: Guide to outlaw Washington, DC.
 HV6795.W3F73 2012
 364.109753—dc23

                                                        2012003158

Printed in the United States of America

10 9 8 7 6 5 4 3 2 1

CONTENTS

"Monsters are real, and ghosts are real too. They live inside us, and sometimes, they win."

—STEPHEN KING

"Evil often triumphs, but never conquers."

—JOSEPH ROUX

CAPITAL CRIMES:
An Introduction

As a child, I saw Washington, D.C., as a sort of Emerald City, a wondrous place where great men gathered to do great deeds in the great halls of our exceptional nation. This city of soaring marble and extraordinary possibilities, in my young mind, was a place where good things happened. I knew from my early fascination with the Lincoln assassination that bad things happened, but I presumed they were exceedingly rare. After all, even Oz had its Wicked Witch and flying monkeys.

Then I grew up. The miasma of the Vietnam War, which dominated my grade-school years, seemed to emanate from Washington like swamp gas. After JFK, Bobby, and King, I began to imagine it as a place where assassins lurked. The final betrayal of Watergate inspired me to become a journalist. The city I once imagined turned upside-down. I began to see our capital city as far more complex, far less noble. The Wizard had bedbugs.

Place matters, even in crime. Being there is not just a good way to understand history, but in some places, it helps you grasp the desperation and loneliness of the people who were there before you, especially in places where our imagination, myth, and history entangle. Places where the past exists just beneath the surface of the present.

This book will take you to the intimate little playhouse where American history was changed by a single bullet. It will let you stand in a hotel where our confidence was shaken—maybe shattered —more than one hundred years later. It will point the way to spots where famous and infamous crime figures—J. Edgar Hoover, Beltway Sniper John Allen Muhammad, assassins John Wilkes Booth and Charles Guiteau, Eliot Ness, and the Black Sox's Chick Gandil, among many others—once stood. And it will take you to places where our crime history took unexpected, momentous, macabre, or even whimsical turns.

So let this book be your window on the past. Our appreciation of history begins in the places where it happened. And now the magic of the Global Positioning System (GPS) allows you to stand in a precise historic spot, as best as our modern technology and imaginations can muster. We have made every attempt to put you within inches of the past.

This is certainly no ordinary guidebook. You won't find many suggestions for places to sleep or eat, although you might often find such spots by chasing these ghosts. Rather, consider this a history book that tells you exactly where to stand to get fleeting glimpses of the past and present—and maybe a bit of the future.

Washington (and its environs) is so full of history that you can hardly walk a block without stepping over it. So slow down and take some time to find it. History is how we know, how we learn. And being there makes all the difference.

—Ron Franscell
San Antonio, Texas

HOW TO USE THIS BOOK

The entries in this book are divided into four chapters: two geographic regions (Washington, D.C., and Maryland) and one segment each about the Lincoln Assassination and Arlington National Cemetery. Each entry has physical and GPS directions that will let you stand in the footsteps of history—not in the general vicinity, but literally on a spot relevant to one of the Washington area's most notable and fascinating crimes or outlaw-related figures.

Crimes big and small have been committed every single day since mankind began to distinguish right from wrong. This book cannot begin to aggregate every injustice, every crime, every inhumanity ever visited upon the nation's capital and its outlying areas, although even the smallest crime certainly affects victims, survivors, and communities as much as the most celebrated crimes in our history. And in some cases here, I have chosen only a few representative sites. So please don't be offended if you feel I've overlooked a crime or site you believe should have been included.

A word of warning: Many of these sites are on private property. Always seek permission before venturing onto private land. Do not trespass. It's rude and illegal, and as we know from Washington's criminal reputation, everybody has a gun or a lawyer.

I made every effort to be precise in my facts and directions, but being human, I am bound to have erred here and there. If you believe I should include a certain crime in future editions—or if you see an error that should be corrected—please send me a note at Ron Franscell, OUTLAW DC, c/o Globe Pequot Press, 246 Goose Lane, PO Box 480, Guilford, CT 06437; or e-mail editorial@globepequot.com.

A NOTE ABOUT GPS ACCURACY

GPS readings are affected by many things, including satellite positions, noise in the radio signal, weather, natural barriers to the signal, and variations between devices. Noise—static, interference, or competing frequencies—can cause errors up to thirty feet. Clouds, bad weather, mountains, or buildings can also skew readings up to one hundred feet.

While I've tried to make every GPS coordinate in *The Crime Buff's Guide to Outlaw Washington, DC* as precise as possible, I can't be sure you'll visit under the same conditions or with the same kind of equipment. The best possible way to get an accurate reading is to be sure the satellites and your receiver have a clear view of each other, with no clouds, trees, or other interference. If your device doesn't bring you to the right spot, look around. It's likely within a few paces.

COVER PHOTO KEY
(All cover photos by the author.)

Top row, left to right:
The Catonsville Nine, page 154
Disgraced Politician William Belknap, page 192
Beltway Sniper, page 166

Middle row, left to right:
Legend of the Bunny Man, page 57
Mysterious Serial Killings, page 152
Terror Attack on Congress, page 76

Bottom row, left to right:
National Museum of Crime and Punishment, page 10
Booth's Escape, page 105
National Law Enforcement Officers Memorial, page 65

1

WASHINGTON, DC
(and related environs)

ROOTS OF A CANNIBALISTIC SERIAL KILLER

The former St. John's Orphanage is now known as George Washington University's Old Main at 1922 F Street NW, or GPS 38.897159, -77.04459.

Albert Fish (1870–1936) was a sick puppy. Students of serial killers recognize him as one of the cruelest and twisted child killers in American history, a real-life Hannibal Lecter who often ate his victims after inflicting unspeakable atrocities.

And it all started during a perverse childhood in Washington.

He was born Hamilton Fish in 1870 to a family with a history of alcoholism and mental illness. Fish's childhood home was on B Street NE (now Constitution Avenue) between Second and Third Streets, around GPS 38.891947, -77.00267. His elderly father, Randall, was a Potomac riverboat skipper who died when Hamilton was only five years old and was buried in Congressional Cemetery (1801 E Street SE in Range 96, Site 89 of the Grand Lodge Grounds, or GPS 38.88197, -76.98049).

So Fish's much younger mother abandoned him to the St. John's Orphanage, where the little boy's life went from bad to worse.

Other boys nicknamed him "Ham and Eggs," which he hated, so he adopted the name of a dead sibling: Albert. Discipline at the orphanage wasn't just strict, it was brutal . . . but little Albert discovered he actually liked the pain. By age twelve, he'd had his first

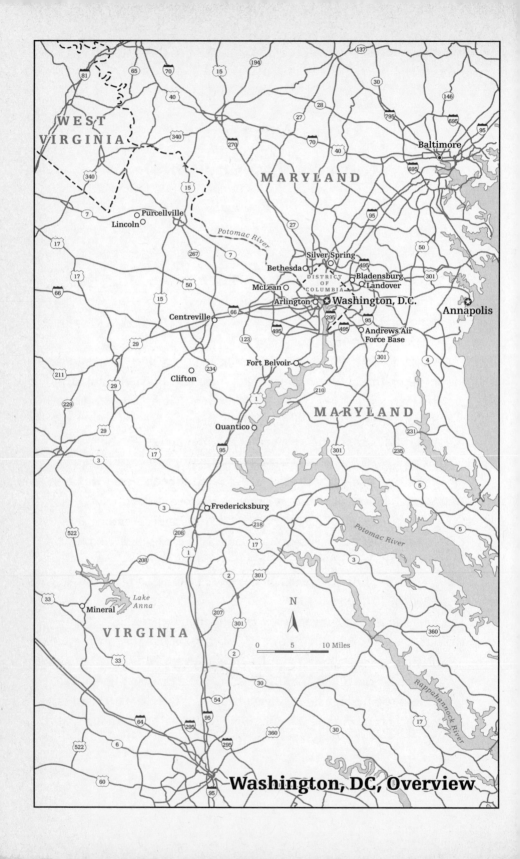

Washington, DC, Overview

homosexual tryst and was introduced to voyeurism, urophagia, and coprophagia (just look them up). By age twenty, he moved to New York City to become a male prostitute and began raping little boys.

Over the next forty-five years, Fish evolved into a sadomasochistic serial killer, cannibal, and child-rapist of the most extreme kind. Accounts of his sexual festishes are too grotesque and startling for polite company. Although he later claimed hundreds of victims, only a handful have ever been confirmed.

Known as the Brooklyn Vampire or the Werewolf of Wysteria, Fish was finally arrested for the 1928 murder of a little girl after he sent a taunting, cruel letter to her parents six years later describing how he killed and ate her over a nine-day period. He was convicted and executed in 1936 at age sixty-five in Sing Sing's electric chair in New York, and his unclaimed body was reportedly buried secretly somewhere on prison grounds.

Sadistic serial killer Albert Fish

INVASION OF THE BODY-SNATCHERS

Ryder's Castle was at 419-423 New Jersey Avenue NW, or GPS 38.895427, -77.010955. It no longer exists, but it was just a few steps from the city's old Police Precinct No. 6, which is now a fire station.

For most of the nineteenth century, American medical schools were opening at a brisk rate, educating doctors for a growing nation. And to teach anatomy, they required a supply of a commodity that wasn't especially rare but was hard to come by: corpses.

Before the Civil War, eighty-five medical colleges were operating in the US—all hungry for fresh cadavers—and body-snatching was illegal in only three states. Records show that some five thousand American corpses were dissected every year by medical students, and most are presumed to have been supplied by shady gangs of body-snatchers. By the time New York passed its "anatomy law" in 1854, up to seven hundred New Yorkers' bodies were disappearing every year. Each corpse might be worth $15 to $25, or about $700 in today's dollars.

The only law in Washington, D.C., against this ghoulish practice was larceny. So if a body-snatcher merely stripped the corpse of its clothing (the only thing deemed worth stealing), he or she was unlikely to face any serious criminal charges.

Grave-robbing became such a problem that in 1878, an Ohio casket-maker sold "torpedo coffins" rigged with small bombs that would explode if anyone trifled with the grave. (Just to be safe, tread lightly in Ohio cemeteries.)

Several body-snatching rings—they preferred the term "resurrectionists"—operated in Washington in the late 1800s. Among the most notable were the brother-and-sister team of Percy and Maud Brown, two Russian immigrants.

The Browns lived in a subterranean warren beneath a frame house near the intersection of Massachusetts Avenue and Third Street NE, described by a visiting *Washington Post* reporter as "a cave for dead bodies." Here, they blithely stored their "product" until they could sell it.

Among the graves they robbed in 1888 (along with many others) was the final resting spot of the recently departed Mrs. Ann R. Smith. Digging up her fresh grave at Mount Olivet Cemetery (1300 Bladensburg Road NE) in Section 14, Lot 143, or GPS 38.91013, -76.98149, they left her clothes in the hole and sold her body to the National Medical College (then at 1335 H Street NW, or GPS 38.900342, -77.031171). A private detective traced the body to a dissecting table at the college, and Percy Brown briefly faced charges before being released for lack of evidence.

But the Browns decided to change addresses. They moved to a building known as Ryder's Castle—several row houses connected by hallways and tunnels—where a small cabal of resurrectionists and other lowlifes operated until the city finally cracked down in the 1890s.

After that, the Browns disappeared. Because no record exists of their deaths, it is possible they legally donated their bodies to science.

JFK PARAMOUR SLAIN

The crime scene is on the Chesapeake and Ohio Canal towpath in Georgetown, at GPS 38.928958, -77.111567.

Mary Pinchot Meyer (1920–1964) was an enigma. Born into a wealthy family of Pennsylvania socialists, the path of her privileged life meandered among some of the most famous people of her day: Justice Louis Brandeis, Mabel Dodge, Katharine Graham, Timothy Leary, Ben Bradlee, and, eventually, a lover named John F. Kennedy.

A Vassar graduate, Mary Pinchot met Marine Lt. Cord Meyer in 1944, and they married a year later. Although Meyer led several left-wing groups after the war, there's evidence he was also working secretly for the CIA. By 1951, he was officially a CIA employee running Operation Mockingbird, designed to influence American media and put many reporters on the CIA payroll. Mary, a sometime journalist, was briefly considered but was ultimately judged to be a risky asset because of her spontaneous love affairs.

In 1954, a new young senator from Massachusetts named John Kennedy and his wife, Jackie, moved into a sprawling estate just down the road from the Meyers' home. Mary and Jackie became quick friends and often walked together. At the same time, Meyer's sister Antoinette had married *Newsweek* reporter (and future *Washington Post* editor) Ben Bradlee.

The Meyers divorced in 1958, and Mary began a series of flings and resumed an abstract-expressionist painting hobby. For a studio, she was given a bungalow on the grounds of the Bradlees' home, the historic Laird-Dunlop House (3014 N Street NW, or GPS 38.90667, -77.05944). Eventually, she moved into a nearby townhouse at 1523 34th Street NW (GPS 38.90936, -77.067767).

In late 1961, the single, charming, and notoriously frisky socialite visited her old friend and now president John Kennedy at the White House. An intimate affair began. She told friends that she and JFK had been together about thirty times and often enjoyed marijuana or LSD that she brought to their trysts.

JFK was assassinated in November 1963. Eleven months later (and two days before her forty-fourth birthday), Mary Pinchot Meyer finished a painting in her borrowed studio and took a walk on the C&O Canal's towpath. Two men changing a tire nearby heard a gunshot, a woman's cry for help, then a second shot. Running to the sounds, one of them saw a black man standing over Mary's body, his pants unzipped.

Moments later, police arrested a black man named Ray Crump near the scene. He was sopping wet and claimed he had gone in the river to retrieve a lost fishing pole (later found at his home). The eyewitness identified Crump as the man he'd seen with Mary's body. The circumstantial case against Crump was strong, but the murder weapon was never found. Crump was eventually acquitted for lack of evidence.

Although Crump went on to a prodigious life of crime with twenty-two arrests in the Washington, D.C., area, including assault with a deadly weapon, arson, and rape, the conspiracy theories sprouted like weeds. When news of her affair with JFK became known, some believed Mary was killed by the CIA to cover up anything she might have known about his assassination. Some have even surmised it was the KGB. Nonetheless, Mary's murder remains officially unsolved.

After a funeral in the National Cathedral (GPS 38.93057, -77.07087), Mary was buried in the Milford Cemetery in Milford, Pennsylvania, where she grew up. Her ex-husband, renowned CIA operative Cord Meyer (1920–2001), is buried in Section 60, Site 7942 (GPS 38.87571, -77.06393) at Arlington National Cemetery.

PRESIDENT RONALD REAGAN SHOT

The Washington Hilton Hotel is at 1919 Connecticut Avenue NW. The president was shot near the T Street NW exit, just west (left) of the portico at GPS 38.9161, -77.045421.

On March 30, 1981—a mere sixty-nine days after he was sworn in—President Ronald Reagan emerged from the Washington Hilton after a speech to a local branch of the AFL-CIO and waved to onlookers. But among the crowd that stopped to see the new president was an assassin.

At 2:27 p.m., a troubled young man named John Hinckley, standing just twenty feet away, fired all six shots in his .22-caliber revolver into the president's entourage, grievously wounding D.C. Metro Police Officer Thomas Delahanty in the back, Secret Service Agent Timothy McCarthy in the belly, and press secretary James Brady in the head. Hinckley's sixth bullet ricocheted off the presidential limousine's door and lodged in President Reagan's left lung, just an inch from his heart.

Four minutes later, Reagan was rushed into the emergency room at George Washington University Medical Center (900 23rd Street NW, or GPS 38.901741, -77.050269). This is where the wounded president famously joked to his distraught wife, "Honey, I forgot to duck," and later quipped to his surgeons, "Please tell me you're all Republicans." But Reagan's humor masked the fact that the seventy-year-old man's breathing was labored, and his internal injuries were bleeding so profusely that he'd lose about half his blood supply in the next twenty-four hours.

Reagan lived, the only sitting American president to survive an assassin's wounds. The emergency room was later renamed the Ronald Reagan Institute of Emergency Medicine in his honor. Delahanty and McCarthy also survived their wounds. Eerily, the assassination attempt came just nine days after the Reagans had visited

Would-be assassin John Hinckley shot President Reagan and three others on this spot outside the Washington Hilton in 1981.

Ford's Theatre (511 Tenth Street NW, or GPS 38.896667, -77.025833), where Abraham Lincoln had been shot 115 years earlier.

James Brady's head wound permanently disabled him and confined him to a wheelchair. He and his wife, Sarah, became active in gun-control issues and, in 2001, a coalition of gun-control lobbies renamed itself the Brady Campaign to Prevent Gun Violence (1225 Eye Street NW, Suite 1100, or GPS 38.901532, -77.029261).

The near-tragedy set in motion the long, strange story of would-be assassin John W. Hinckley, a troubled twenty-four-year-old man who nursed an unhealthy obsession with actress Jodie Foster. Hoping to impress Foster (who'd played a teen hooker in the movie *Taxi Driver*, in which a troubled young man tries to assassinate a politician), Hinckley made his plans to kill Reagan.

He arrived in Washington by bus the day before, then checked into Room 312 at the Park Central Hotel near the White House (1800 G Street NW, or GPS 38.898188, -77.041814). The next morning, he wrote a letter to Foster explaining his impending "historical deed," left it in his hotel room, then took a cab to the Washington Hilton.

After the shooting, Hinckley was found not guilty by reason of insanity, sparking a national debate over the insanity defense. He was committed to St. Elizabeth's Hospital (1100 Alabama Avenue SE, or GPS 38.8492, -76.9896), where he could be released as soon as a federal judge believes he has been cured of his obsession with Foster, his schizophrenia, and depression. He enjoys occasional unsupervised visits with family and friends outside the hospital, and he has even married twice while institutionalized.

In 2011, a forensic psychologist told the court, "Hinckley has recovered to the point that he poses no imminent risk of danger to himself or others."

For a detailed historical account of the assassination attempt, see Del Quentin Wilber's 2011 book, *Rawhide Down*.

See also Lincoln Assassination chapter, and "Assassination Archives and Research Center" (this chapter).

NATIONAL MUSEUM OF CRIME AND PUNISHMENT

The museum is at 575 Seventh Street NW (half a block south of the Gallery Place-Chinatown Metro station) or GPS 38.896747, -77.021799. It is primarily open 10 a.m. to 7 p.m. daily, but hours vary by season. Admission charged; www.crimemuseum.org.

"Old Smokey," the Tennessee electric chair that executed 125 killers from 1916 to 1960, is displayed at the Museum of Crime and Punishment.

This privately owned, 28,000-square-foot museum explores the colorful history of American criminology and penology in America, from pirates to gunslingers to gangsters to white-collar criminals. Visitors can see Tennessee's "Old Smokey" electric chair and a colonial pillory, experience driving and shooting simulations, and learn real-life CSI techniques in a crime lab. No funky roadside attraction, this upscale museum has a load of fascinating artifacts, from a real Colt police revolver and serial killer John Wayne Gacy's oil paints to a wax figure of the G-Man himself, J. Edgar Hoover.

Co-owned by TV's John Walsh, the three-floor museum also houses the studios for *America's Most Wanted.*

9/11 PENTAGON MEMORIAL

This memorial is at 1 Rotary Road, beside the western wall of the Pentagon, at GPS 38.869788, -77.059414. It is open twenty-four hours a day every day of the week. Free admission.

On September 11, 2001, American Airlines Flight 77 slammed directly into the western wall of the Pentagon (at approximately GPS 38.871061, -77.058213). Not counting the Islamic radicals who had hijacked the jet, 184 people died.

This somber memorial, opened on September 11, 2008, features 184 lighted benches, each engraved with a victim's name, arranged across 1.93 acres in order of the victims' ages, starting with three-year-old Dana Falkenberg and ending with seventy-one-year-old John Yamnicky Sr. As you read each victim's name, you will be facing the plane's fatal path. Benches facing the Pentagon commemorate people killed inside.

One piece of charred limestone from the pierced Pentagon wall was incorporated into the renovations.

All but five of the victims were identified. The cremated ashes of those who were unidentified were placed in a single casket and buried within view of the Pentagon beneath a five-sided granite marker bearing the 184 names. For more about that memorial, please see the Arlington National Cemetery chapter.

This somber memorial commemorates the 184 men, women, and children who died in the 9/11 terror attack at the Pentagon.

FUTURE BLACK SOX RINGLEADER'S HOME

The Maxwell apartment building is at 1419 Clifton NW, or GPS 38.922755, -77.032733.

In 1912, the Washington Senators signed a rising minor-league first baseman named Arnold "Chick" Gandil, who proved to be just what the hapless team needed. Over the next 117 games in 1912, he batted .305 and led all American League first basemen in fielding.

And he got even better in 1913, when he hit his career-high average of .318. Over the next few years, he became the slugging heart of the Senators' offense and extremely popular with home fans at Washington's Griffith Stadium (demolished in 1965 and now the site of Howard University Hospital at the corner of Georgia Avenue and W Street NW, or GPS 38.9175, -77.020278).

Gandil led a celebrity's life. He lived in Apartment 11 at The Maxwell, a luxury apartment building in the city's upscale Columbia Heights neighborhood. He also invested in some local businesses, including a bowling alley in the Arcade Building at 3134 14th Street NW (GPS 38.929304, -77.03281). The popular amusement center—with theaters, dance hall, soda fountain, a market, billiards, and more—came long before today's indoor malls. Razed in 1948, it is now the site of . . . an indoor mall.

He also befriended Joseph "Sport" Sullivan, a Boston gambler and bookie, who cultivated relationships with ballplayers to harvest profitable inside information.

But in 1916, the Senators sold Gandil to the Cleveland Indians, who in turn sold him in 1917 to the Chicago White Sox, who hoped Gandil would lead them to a World Series that year. But the chronic malcontent Gandil played without any special luster in 1917 and 1918.

Gandil's life changed in 1919. Most baseball historians agree Gandil approached his old bookie buddy Sport Sullivan with a wild proposal: If gamblers would pay big money, Gandil promised to arrange for his heavily favored team to lose the World Series.

Gandil recruited six other players—including superstar "Shoeless" Joe Jackson—to accept gamblers' money to throw the 1919 Series with the weaker Cincinnati Reds. The game-fixers eventually received far less money than they had been promised, although Gandil reportedly pocketed $35,000 in bribes. A 1921 criminal trial in Chicago acquitted the seven White Sox players—plus one who knew about the fix but didn't participate—but baseball commissioner Kenesaw Mountain Landis still banned all the players, including Gandil, for life. The "eight men out" became known as the Black Sox.

Gandil (1888–1970) played secretly under assumed names for various bush-league teams and eventually retired to a quiet life as a plumber who wanted to be known for fixing leaky pipes, not baseball games. In 1970, he died at age eighty-three in Calistoga, California, and he was buried quietly in the St. Helena Cemetery (2461 Spring Street, St Helena, California, in Row 20) before the world learned that one of baseball's greatest cheaters had died.

See also "A Ride on the Legal Carousel," Glen Echo (Maryland).

LINDBERGH BABY SCAM VICTIM

Rock Creek Cemetery is at Rock Creek Church Road NW and Webster Street NW. Evalyn Walsh McLean's mausoleum is in Section 14 at GPS 38.946935, -77.012757.

When the toddler son of heroic aviator Charles Lindbergh was kidnapped from his crib in New Jersey in March 1932, it was instantly dubbed America's most heinous crime ever. The intrigues that followed—ransom notes, clandestine meetings in cemeteries, even a fictional investigation by comic-page cop Dick Tracy—kept headlines and newsreels crackling for months and fixated the public.

Less than a week after the curly-haired baby went missing, Evalyn Walsh McLean, a fabulously rich Washington socialite and owner of the Hope Diamond, summoned a sometime federal agent (and bootlegger) named Gaston Means to her lavish home with a proposition: She'd bankroll an undercover operation to expose the kidnappers by using Means's contacts in the crime underworld. The professional swindler Means was only too happy to take the assignment . . . and McLean's money.

McLean gave Means $100,000 for ransom money, and he later asked for another $4,000 to cover the kidnappers' expenses while he concocted a complicated scheme of code names and cross-country junkets. He assured McLean the baby was alive and well. Even Lindbergh himself believed Means was in contact with the kidnappers and that his son would soon be returned.

But the baby was never returned. When Means asked for another $35,000, the frustrated McLean asked for her money back—and Means promptly disappeared.

Evalyn Walsh McLean, a wealthy socialite duped by con artists in the Lindbergh baby case, lies in this mausoleum.

A little more than two months after the kidnapping, the baby's decomposed corpse was discovered less than a mile from the Lindbergh home. In 1935, a carpenter named Richard Bruno Hauptmann was convicted of the baby's murder and was executed in 1936.

The con man Means was eventually captured, convicted of grand larceny, and sent to Leavenworth Federal Penitentiary, where he died in 1938. The money was never recovered.

McLean, whose family had been rocked by tragedies that some attributed to the "curse" of her Hope Diamond, died in 1947 at age sixty from pneumonia. Her sprawling forty-three-acre estate, known as Friendship, where she met Gaston Means for the first time, was torn down and redeveloped into apartments and condos (3811 Porter Street NW, or GPS 38.93761, -77.075164). Only the home's original ballroom remains.

Since 1958, the Hope Diamond has been owned and displayed by the Smithsonian Institution's Museum of Natural History (at the intersection of Tenth Street and Constitution Avenue NW, or GPS 38.891111, -77.025833).

EXORCIST STEPS
This haunting stairway is right across M Street NW from the Key Bridge, at GPS 38.905473, -77.070202.

These claustrophobic, vertiginous ninety-seven steps in Georgetown were long known as the Hitchcock Steps, even though the horror master never filmed anything there.

But after 1973, they became famous as the "Exorcist Steps" because of the haunting role they played in one of the scariest horror movies ever made.

Yes, this is the exact spot in William Friedkin's classic *The Exorcist* where the fictional Father Damien Karras (Jason Miller) throws himself from a possessed little girl's bedroom window and tumbles to his death down these steep stairs in an attempt to foil the demons.

A few steps from the stairs is 3600 Prospect Street (GPS 38.905774, -77.070438), the redbrick house where the demonized Regan MacNeil (Linda Blair) lived.

But here's the scary part: William Peter Blatty's original novel was based on a real-life exorcism that happened nearby in Maryland in 1949. See also "Story behind *The Exorcist*," Cottage City (Maryland).

This steep flight of stairs made an ominous appearance as a crime scene in The Exorcist.

JIM MORRISON'S FIRST PERFORMANCE

The former site of Coffee 'n' Confusion is at 945 K Street NW, at GPS 38.90266, -77.025334.

Long before Jim Morrison became the iconic (and occasionally exhibitionist) lead singer for The Doors, a 1960s rock band known for its dark, poetic cuts, he was a quiet teenager who haunted a little Beatnik coffee house in Washington called Coffee 'n' Confusion.

And almost a decade before Morrison was famously convicted of exposing his private parts to a Miami audience, he gave his first-ever public performance at that café . . . minus the fleshy bits.

One night in 1960, near the end of his junior year in high school, Morrison recited one of his own poems in his largely forgotten debut. Biographer Mark Opsasnick believes Morrison read an early version of "Horse Latitudes," which later became a Doors song.

Morrison graduated from George Washington High School in 1961 and UCLA in 1965 before forming a bluesy, psychedelic rock band called The Doors with his pal Ray Manzarek. In 1969, a drug-fueled Morrison reportedly unzipped and flashed his audience, for which he was convicted of indecent exposure and profanity in one of rock 'n' roll's most infamous criminal acts. He never served a day in jail before he died in 1971 at age twenty-seven of a drug overdose in Paris.

In 2010, almost forty years later, the Florida Board of Executive Clemency voted unanimously to posthumously pardon Morrison.

GHOST OF THE NATIONAL THEATRE

The National Theatre is at 1321 Pennsylvania Avenue NW, or GPS 38.896264, -77.030786.

Players at the National Theatre still whisper about the ghost of a murdered actor that legend says was buried in the dirt beneath the modern-day stage. Fact or fable? Well, as Shakespeare's Hamlet said, "The play's the thing."

And the story of ill-fated Shakespearean actor John Edward McCullough has been playing secretly at the National for more than one hundred years. The story goes like this:

In the late 1800s, a creek flowed through an open raceway under the stage floor, an ideal wash basin for poor actors to wash their costumes and clothes. One day, McCullough and a fellow thespian got into an argument down there. Some say it was over an actress, others say it was about a plum role they both wanted.

Either way, shots were fired. McCullough fell dead in that cellar, and his body was hastily buried in the dirt floor—or so the myth says.

Nobody knew much about McCullough's sudden disappearance, much less his clandestine grave, but people soon began spying McCullough's ghost in the theater, and a legend was born.

In the 1930s, Washington detectives proposed to excavate the dirt floor, but clannish, superstitious theater people revolted, and it never happened. However, when the theater was refurbished in 1984, the legend got new life when a rusty, 1800s pistol was found in the dirt under the stage and donated to the Smithsonian.

Nice story, but McCullough was not murdered. Although one of the most celebrated tragedians of his day, he developed dementia and was committed to an insane asylum in Philadelphia, where he died in 1885 at age fifty-three. He was buried in Mount Moriah Cemetery in Philadelphia under what is said to be the tallest monument ever built to an actor.

A WAR CRIMINAL IS HANGED

Mount Olivet Cemetery is at 1300 Bladensburg Road NE. Captain Henry Wirz's grave is in Section 27 at GPS 38.90899, -76.97925.

The Confederates called it Camp Sumter, but the Union soldiers who suffered in the Georgia POW camp called it Andersonville.

The twenty-six-acre, open-air stockade was only used for fifteen months, but almost fifty thousand Union prisoners lived there amid appalling and brutal conditions—and thirteen thousand of them died from malnutrition, exposure, and disease, and were buried nearby in a mass grave.

Ironically, Andersonville's commandant was a Swiss-born medical doctor, Captain Henry Wirz. When *Harper's Weekly* published photos of the prisoners and the camp after the war, Northerners were enraged. Wirz was tried as a war criminal.

Although Wirz claimed he had begged his commanders for more food and medicine, Yankee POWs recounted how he often warned

Commandant of the infamous Confederate prison camp known as Andersonville, Henry Wirz was executed for war crimes after the Civil War.

that if any prisoner escaped, he would "starve every damn Yankee for it." His defense—which echoed in the Nuremberg War Crimes trials eighty years later—was that he was only following orders.

Wirz (1823–1865) was convicted of war crimes and four days later, he was hanged in the same Old Capitol Prison yard where Lincoln's conspirators had been hanged. While executioners placed a black hood over his head, a chant rose among the onlooking solders: "Wirz. Remember. Andersonville."

The hanging site is now beneath the US Supreme Court building (1 First Street NE, or GPS 38.890633, -77.005183).

Most of Wirz's corpse was buried unceremoniously with the Lincoln conspirators' corpses in the Old Arsenal Prison Yard (now Fort McNair, at GPS 38.866556, -77.017095), but his head and other parts were hacked off to be displayed. What remained was exhumed in 1869 and moved to Mount Olivet Cemetery, where Lincoln conspirator Mary Surratt is also buried.

The burial ground at Andersonville is now a national cemetery.

A DRUG DEAL GONE GOOD

Lafayette Square Park is just north of the White House, between Pennsylvania Avenue and H Street NW at GPS 38.899422, -77.036583.

In September 1989, President George H. W. Bush went on TV to unveil a new get-tough antidrug message. To punctuate his message, he displayed a baggie of crack cocaine that had been bought across the street from the White House that afternoon in Lafayette Square Park.

One little problem: DEA agents had lured a local drug dealer to the park just so the president could have an arresting "fact" for his nationally televised speech. Agents later revealed that the setup was harder than you might think: The crack dealer didn't know where the White House was.

THE RACKETS OF FOGGY BOTTOM

The Warrings' headquarters were at 2423 Pennsylvania Avenue NW at GPS 38.903503, -77.052315.

A lot of professional mobsters have done quite well in Washington without holding any public office. Among them, the numbers-running Warring brothers.

Emmitt "Little Man" Warring, with siblings Leo Paul and Charlie "Rags" Warring, started as rum-running bootleggers but took over the D.C. numbers racket during the 1930s and '40s. Their base was a third-floor room at this site near Washington Circle, but they had a tight grip on all the rackets in Foggy Bottom and Georgetown. At the height of the Depression, they were reportedly raking in over $2 million a year and employed dozens.

Indicted for tax evasion in 1938, the brothers eventually pled guilty after three circuslike trials, but their rackets continued to make millions well into the 1940s.

"Little Man" Warring died in 1974 and is buried at Mount Olivet Cemetery, 1300 Bladensburg Road NE. His unmarked grave is in Section 18 at GPS 38.90902, -76.98047.

WHITE SHEETS IN WASHINGTON

The Washington Monument is on the National Mall at GPS 38.889468, -77.03524.

From tax protesters to TV comedians, all kinds of people have been marching on Washington for well over one hundred years. About the only thing they've had in common are wildly differing estimates of crowd size.

On August 8, 1925, the Ku Klux Klan mounted a march that captured national attention. An estimated forty thousand white-robed Klansmen (the KKK claimed three hundred thousand) paraded silently down Pennsylvania Avenue to gather around the base of the

Washington Monument for rousing speeches against blacks, Jews, and Catholics, among others. Although the KKK was linked to terrible crimes against its enemies, the march unfolded without any serious incidents.

Legendary *Baltimore Sun* reporter H. L. Mencken stood behind armed Marines on the steps of the US Treasury and watched the parade pass for almost four hours. The *Washington Post* reported the next day that "the size and nature" of the march shocked normally unshockable Washington. It also noted that the parade was filled with children and "almost as many women as men."

Although the reconstituted KKK had as many as three million members in the 1920s—about half in American cities—the Washington march marked its high-water mark.

See also "'Monkey Trial' Reporter's Home," Baltimore (Maryland).

PHILANDERING SENATOR MURDERED
The site of the former Raleigh Hotel is on the northeast corner of 12th Street and Pennsylvania Avenue NW, or GPS 38.895207, -77.027821.

Arthur Brown (1843–1906) was one of the first two US senators from the new state of Utah in 1896—and the only member of Congress ever murdered by a jealous mistress.

Even before he was elected, the married Salt Lake City lawyer was known to harbor grudges and a defective moral compass.

A renowned lothario, Brown had several mistresses, including Anne Bradley, a woman half his age. Their torrid, well-publicized affair lasted long after Brown had left the Senate.

Brown repeatedly promised he'd divorce his wife (also a former mistress), but it never happened. In December 1906, the lovesick Bradley followed Brown on a trip to Washington, where she found a secret stash of love letters that suggested he was about to marry another woman. Enraged, she shot Brown in the belly in his Raleigh Hotel room. He died four days later at Emergency Hospital. He is buried in Utah.

Bradley faced murder charges but was acquitted.

DR. MICHAEL HALBERSTAM MURDER
The Halberstam house is at 2806 Battery Place NW, or GPS 38.926182, -77.097751. This is private property.

Late on December 5, 1980, Dr. Michael Halberstam, a prominent Washington cardiologist, author, and brother of Pulitzer Prize–winning author David Halberstam, surprised a burglar in his suburban home. Halberstam, shot twice in the chest by the fleeing burglar, jumped into his car with his wife and sped toward nearby Sibley Hospital, but on the way he saw the burglar on a neighborhood sidewalk. "That's the guy!" Halberstam shouted as he swerved to hit the thief, who was slightly injured.

Halberstam's car hit a tree and paramedics rushed him to the hospital, but he died on the operating table. He was forty-eight.

The burglar was famous, too. Escaped felon Bernard Welch was one of the FBI's most wanted criminals. He had burgled thousands of houses on his way to becoming known as the Standard Time Burglar, who struck between November and April, when nights were darker and longer, sometimes raping or hog-tying his terrified victims. Police estimate Welch had stolen as much as $20 million in goods between 1965 and 1980; even the gun he used to kill Halberstam had been stolen from an FBI agent. Although busted more than twenty-five times in his life, Welch had lived the good life and invested his stolen riches wisely.

Welch was convicted of Halberstam's murder and received nine consecutive life terms. He escaped once, but was recaptured. He died in federal prison in 1998 at age fifty-eight.

CONGRESSMAN KILLS US ATTORNEY

The murder scene near the northeast corner of Madison Place and Pennsylvania Avenue NW (GPS 38.898925, -77.035014) was covered when the US Treasury Annex was built in 1919.

If this murder had happened today instead of 1859, it would have been at the top of every front page, crime website, and cable newscast for months. A womanizing congressman, a powerful White House insider, a beautiful and adulterous wife, a daylight murder on a city street, breathtaking legal maneuvers . . . it was a tabloid sensation before tabloids were invented.

Dan Sickles was a New York congressman with a bad temper and an eye for the ladies. His wife, Teresa, was a twenty-two-year-old beauty and a rising socialite. And Sickles's bachelor friend Philip Barton Key—son of "The Star-Spangled Banner" lyricist Francis Scott Key—had parlayed his ties with President James Buchanan into an appointment as the US Attorney for Washington.

One day, an anonymous tipster alerted Sickles that his wife was secretly cavorting with Key. When he confronted her, she admitted the affair in a lengthy, salacious written confession, but she didn't warn Key that their secret was out.

So the next day, when Key appeared in Lafayette Park outside Sickles's home and waved his handkerchief in the lovers' secret signal, the cuckolded congressman rushed out with his pistol.

Sickles shot the unarmed Key twice before being subdued by a passerby. Key was taken to the nearby Benjamin Ogle Tayloe House (21 Madison Place NW, or GPS 38.8997, -77.034953), where he died. Only forty, Key was buried in Washington's Oak Hill Cemetery, 3001 R Street NW. His grave is in Lot 834, or GPS 38.91306, -77.05660. A cenotaph in Baltimore's Westminster Burial Ground, 519 West Fayette Street, also pays tribute to Key (GPS 39.28971, -76.623338).

If a Sunday afternoon murder in Victorian-era Washington wasn't enough excitement, the trial was even more explosive.

Sickles became the first criminal defendant ever to use the "temporary insanity" defense, as well as asserting a husband's right to protect the sanctity of his marriage. His legal team included Edwin M. Stanton, Lincoln's future secretary of war. After days of scandalous testimony and courtroom oratory, a jury took little more than an hour to acquit Sickles.

Sickles's political career was savaged, although he became a Union general in the Civil War. His reputation was redeemed in 1863 when he lost his right leg to a rebel cannonball at Gettysburg. He promptly donated the amputated leg to the Army Medical Museum in Washington (now the National Museum of Health and Medicine, 6900 Georgia Avenue and Elder Street NW, or GPS 38.976389, -77.0325), where the bones are still displayed today. The museum is open 10 a.m. to 5:30 p.m. every day except Christmas; free admission.

Teresa died of tuberculosis in 1867 at age thirty-one and was buried in the Brooklyn (New York) Green-Wood Cemetery.

The one-legged Sickles died in 1914 at the ripe old age of ninety-four. He is buried in Arlington National Cemetery (Section 3, Grave 1906, or GPS 38.87339, -77.07140).

See also "A Murderous Congressman" in the Arlington National Cemetery chapter.

DIRTY PHONE CALLS . . . FROM THE IVORY TOWER
The President's Building of American University is on the campus at 4400 Massachusetts Avenue NW. It sits at GPS 38.939078, -77.088377.

When women in suburban Fairfax County, Virginia, first started getting obscene phone calls at home in 1990, the cops didn't exactly mobilize a task force. But one of the women—a cop's wife—decided to take matters into her own hands and asked that the calls be traced.

Incredibly, the calls were coming from the American University campus. More specifically, from the administration building. And particularly, from the university president's office.

Richard Berendzen, AU's president and a Harvard-educated astronomer, abruptly resigned and checked himself into Johns Hopkins Hospital. He was charged with two misdemeanors ("using indecent language while engaging in conversation over the telephone"). He was given two suspended thirty-day sentences and ordered to continue therapy.

In 1993, after returning to American University as a physics professor, Berendzen wrote *Come Here: A Man Overcomes the Tragic Aftermath of Childhood Sexual Abuse,* blaming his phone fetish on an incestuous childhood relationship with his mother. He retired in 2006, although he continued his work as director of NASA's Space Grant Consortium in Washington, D.C.

THE ODESSA FILE

The former Club Madre was at 2204 14th Street NW, or GPS 38.919431, -77.03211.

Odessa Madre was bigger than life. She grew up in the black ghettoes on the poor side of town, but for fifty years—starting in the 1930s—she was one of the District's most flamboyant, resourceful, and successful organized-crime figures.

Eventually known as the "Al Capone of Washington," Madre controlled a good chunk of the local drug trade, ran several brothels, bootlegged liquor, and competed profitably in the gambling and numbers rackets. Over almost five decades, Madre was busted thirty times on fifty-seven charges and spent seven years in prison, but she still got fabulously rich. And the crown jewel in her nefarious kingdom was her headquarters, Club Madre.

Club Madre was a rollicking nightclub in its day. Big-name acts such as Nat King Cole, Count Basie, and Moms Mabley performed there. Patrons often saw Madre sweep into the room with an entourage of her "girls" and sit at a table decorated with fresh red roses. Some say she would set out bowls of cocaine and marijuana at her elaborate parties.

In 1952, the crime-busting Kefauver Committee alleged that a shocking amount of "protection" money was being paid to local cops, and much of it was being channeled through Madre, who eventually retired from her life of crime.

"You say was it worth it? Child, you wonder does crime pay? I'll tell you, yes," she told the *Washington Post* before she died. "It pays a helluva lot of money. And money is something. I don't care who you are, when you got money you can get a lot of doors open because there's always some larcenous heart who's gonna listen to you. And when you show 'em that money . . . if you got a wad, honey, they'll suck up to ya like you was a Tootsie Roll."

Nevertheless, Odessa Madre died penniless in 1990 at age eighty-three. Friends paid her $51 funeral bill. She was buried at Landover's National Harmony Memorial Park, 7101 Sheriff Road. Her unmarked grave is in the Lily Section, Grave 80, or GPS 38.90471, -76.88284.

THE PALMER BOMBING
The bombed house still exists at 2132 R Street NW, or GPS 38.912492, -77.048227.

On June 2, 1919, a violent anarchist accidentally killed himself when he bombed the home of new US Attorney General A. Mitchell Palmer—part of a series of related attacks on government officials across the nation.

The bomb exploded on Palmer's front porch, shattering windows but hurting nobody except the bomber himself. The blast rattled Palmer's neighbors, including a young assistant secretary of the Navy Franklin Delano Roosevelt and his wife, Eleanor, who lived across the street at 2131 R Street NW (GPS 38.912719, -77.048148).

The attacks sent a fearsome shudder through America, still edgy about the Bolshevik revolution in Russia, violent labor strikes, and a deadly flu pandemic that killed nearly a million Americans. Palmer, a possible presidential candidate in 1920, created a secretive intelligence bureau in the Justice Department and placed a young lawyer named J. Edgar Hoover in charge.

Within months, the new Bureau of Investigation was raiding lairs of suspected radicals and deporting "undesirables." Emboldened by his success and the recent Sedition Act, Hoover mounted a massive simultaneous raid on radicals in eight American cities in 1920 and arrested more than six thousand suspected anarchists in one fell swoop. Although today's FBI credits the so-called Palmer Raids with providing valuable experience in intelligence-gathering and terrorism investigation, it also acknowledges the raids were fraught with obvious constitutional and civil-liberty missteps.

The ambitious Palmer forged ahead, predicting that a communist revolution would erupt in the US on May 1, 1920. The American public panicked . . . but the revolution never happened. Not surprisingly, Palmer failed to win the Democratic presidential nomination that year and largely became a footnote in history. He died in 1936 and is buried at Laurelwood Cemetery in Stroudsburg, Pennsylvania.

THE ROOTS OF AN R&B TRAGEDY

Marvin Gaye Park (once known as Watts Branch Park) is a 1.6-mile park that follows a creek in the southeastern part of the District. The amphitheater is at the southeast corner of Foote Street and Division Avenue NE, or GPS 38.896665, -76.92569.

Soul singer Marvin Gaye (1939–1984) might have been a soul divided, but his roots were in the projects of Washington.

He grew up at #12 60th Street NE (a house that no longer exists at GPS 38.890504, -76.915487), in the Washington projects known as the East Capitol Dwellings . . . and he learned to sing in his father's church choir.

Marvin Gay Sr. (his son added the "e" to his stage name) was an iron-fisted, acerbic preacher for a passionate Pentecostal offshoot known as the House of God. His base was a church at 1310 East Capitol Street NE (GPS 38.890005, -76.98777), although he often delivered his sermons in his house or storefronts. At home, he was a mercilessly abusive autocrat who believed he could beat evil out of anyone, especially his own children.

In the 1960s, young Marvin left the ghetto for the bright lights of Motown, where he racked up a string of hits such as "Can I Get a Witness" (1963), "I Heard It Through the Grapevine" (1968), "Mercy Mercy Me" (1971), and "Sexual Healing" (1982). But along the way, he also racked up a raging cocaine habit.

Increasingly paranoid, Gaye feared that unknown people intended to harm his family, so he sent a bodyguard to deliver a handgun to his father, who had moved to a Los Angeles suburb.

Although Gaye was the ruling prince of Motown and had won Grammys, his drug abuse was killing him and intensifying his erratic behavior. So after his world tour ended, Gaye moved into his parents' Culver City home, where he continued his drug bingeing.

On April 1, 1984—one day short of his forty-fifth birthday—a drugged-up Marvin Gaye Jr. intervened in an argument between his parents and pushed his father. A few minutes later, Marvin Gay Sr. shot his son dead with the gift pistol. Later, Gaye's ashes were scattered at sea.

Gay Sr. was charged with first-degree murder but confessed to manslaughter in a plea bargain. He served five years of probation and died of pneumonia in a rest home at age eighty-four in 1998. He is buried at Holy Cross Cemetery in Culver City, California.

Gaye was inducted posthumously into the Rock and Roll Hall of Fame in 1987. His hometown of Washington recognized his influence by renaming Watts Branch Park on the eastern edge of the

District—not far from the projects where Gaye grew up—as Marvin Gaye Park in 2006. Today, the park also features a performing space known as the Marvin Gaye Amphitheater.

UNIVERSITY REGISTRAR'S MURDER

Alma Preinkert's home is at 1436 Chapin Street, or GPS 38.921428, -77.033782.

The illusion of safety in Washington's middle-class neighborhoods in the 1950s was shattered when a beloved academic was slain in her bedroom by a mysterious intruder.

Alma Preinkert (1896–1954) was the enormously popular and exuberant registrar at the University of Maryland. But in the wee hours of February 28, 1954, she was stabbed to death in her second-floor bedroom by a burglar who propped a stolen ladder against her house, jimmied the window lock, and began ransacking the room. Preinkert was stabbed in the ensuing struggle, and her killer fled into the darkness, leaving behind a single gold tie clip.

Washington's top homicide detectives were assigned to the case, hundreds of people were interviewed, and a large reward was posted . . . but the killer has never been found. Preinkert's murder remains on the Metropolitan Police Department's cold-case files.

Thousands of students attended her funeral, and Preinkert was buried not far from her home, in Glenwood Cemetery, 2219 Lincoln Road NE. Her grave is in Section A, Lot 193, or GPS 38.92105, -77.00593.

J. EDGAR HOOVER

Congressional Cemetery is at 1801 E Street SE. The grave is in Range 20, Site 117, or GPS 38.88173, -76.97727.

John Edgar Hoover (1895–1972) was a native Washingtonian, a relative rarity among the many powerful people who have lived here. Certainly none of the eight presidents he served in almost fifty years as head of the FBI could make that claim.

Hoover was born to a doting father and disciplinarian mother in the Seward Square neighborhood three blocks from the US Capitol. In fact, he lived in the family home at 413 Seward Square SE (now a church parking lot at GPS 38.885431, -77.000081) with his widowed mother until she died when he was forty-three—when he had already been the director of the FBI for fourteen years.

Hoover was buried in a lead-lined casket
weighing a half-ton . . . to discourage desecrators.

Nicknamed "Speed," Hoover was valedictorian at Central High School (now Cardozo High School, 1300 Clifton Street NW, GPS 38.9219, -77.0284) and later took night classes in law at George Washington University before being admitted to the bar in 1917.

Two years later, he was hired as an assistant to US Attorney General A. Mitchell Palmer and soon was heading the new General Intelligence Division, which ultimately morphed into the Federal Bureau of Investigation. (See "The Palmer Bombing" in this chapter.) At age twenty-nine, Hoover was the FBI's first director, a job he'd hold for forty-eight years.

During that time as America's top crime-fighter, Hoover formed the nation's first central crime information center and crime lab, formalized police training, made federal agents more professional, and created his famous Ten Most Wanted List . . . all while pursuing (and often catching) Depression-era gangsters such as the Barker Gang, John Dillinger, Pretty Boy Floyd, Machine Gun Kelly, and

J. Edgar Hoover

Al Capone. During World War II, the FBI's focus shifted to anti-communist and espionage targets, then eventually to domestic unrest related to war protests and civil rights in the 1950s and '60s. And Hoover's power only grew.

In 1928, a young Iowan named Clyde Tolson became an FBI agent, and within three years he was Hoover's right-hand man. For the next forty years, they were inseparable. They even shared lunch every workday for forty years, most often at the Mayflower Hotel's Rib Room (now Café Promenade, 1127 Connecticut Avenue NW, or GPS 38.90453, -77.040223).

The FBI's headquarters are named for the agency's legendary director, J. Edgar Hoover.

In 1938, still a bachelor, Hoover moved to 4936 30th Place NW (formerly numbered 4926, at GPS 38.954509, -77.062609), where he had bulletproof windows installed. Tolson continued to live in a separate apartment elsewhere.

When Hoover died in 1972, he was buried beside his parents in a lead-lined coffin that weighed a half-ton to discourage desecrators. He also left his half-million-dollar estate to Tolson, who moved into the house on 30th Place. Some say he seldom left the house except to visit Hoover's grave, and when Tolson died in 1975, he was buried only about a dozen spaces away from Hoover (Range 20, Site 156, or GPS 38.88139, -76.97735).

Today, the FBI's sprawling headquarters (935 Pennsylvania Avenue NW, or GPS 38.894368, -77.024369) are named the J. Edgar Hoover Building.

Many of Hoover's papers, photos, books, and other possessions are housed at the J. Edgar Hoover Center for Law Enforcement, 1733 16th Street NW (GPS 38.913715, -77.036093). The room is open to the public during normal business hours and is closed on weekends.

Hoover's legacy is a mixed bag. While he built the world's most famous and effective crime-fighting force, he also often overstepped his limits and abused his power. Stories about his alleged cross-dressing have largely been debunked, although hard-to-ignore rumors that started in the 1920s about his sexual preferences persist today. Many books have been written about Hoover, including Curt Gentry's 1991 *J. Edgar Hoover: The Man and the Secrets* and Ronald Kessler's 2003 *The Bureau: The Secret History of the FBI.* Hoover is also portrayed in Clint Eastwood's 2011 biopic, *J. Edgar.*

Also in Congressional Cemetery:

- The dapper **Colonel Beau Hickman** (1813–1873) was one of the District's most famed con men. Although a notorious gambler and grifter, when he died penniless in his hotel room, he was buried in a pauper's grave, shocking his friends (whom, according to a lengthy obituary in the *Washington Evening Star,* he never fleeced). One night, Hickman's buddies decided to dig him up for a more proper burial but were startled to find that body-snatchers had beaten them to the grave and removed many of the decomposing Colonel's parts. "Turning their faces to the wind and taking a deep breath" (a local newspaper reported), they gathered up what was left and tossed it in the back of a buckboard. Racing through Washington's dark streets, they arrived at Congressional Cemetery, dug a hasty grave and dumped the Colonel in it. He's still there (Range 88, Site 125, or GPS 38.88168, -76.98015).

- **William P. Wood** (1820–1903) the first chief of the US Secret Service, which was established in the wake of Lincoln's assassination but was primarily intended to fight counterfeiting. Wood died a pauper, but in 2001 retired Secret Service agents raised enough money to put a monument over his grave. Wood's grave is in Range 65, Site 248, or GPS 38.88052, -76.97929.

- Lincoln conspirator **David Herold** (1842–1865), who was hanged for his key role in the assassination of President Lincoln. He's buried in his sister Elizabeth Herold's grave in Range 46, Site 44, or GPS 38.88235, -76.97838. See more in the chapter about the Lincoln assassination.

- **Randall Fish** (1795–1875), father of serial killer Albert Fish. His grave is in Range 96, Site 89 of the Grand Lodge Grounds, or GPS 38.88197, -76.98049). See "Roots of a Cannibalistic Serial Killer" in this chapter.

- A cenotaph here pays tribute to Congressman **Jonathan Cilley** of Maine, who was killed by another congressman in an 1838 duel that led to a Washington law against challenging anyone to a duel. The marker is in Range 30, Site 60, at GPS 38.88221, -76.97769, although the thirty-six-year-old politician was buried in Elm Grove Cemetery in Thomaston, Maine.

- Former Attorney General **William Wirt** and renowned Washington madam **Mary Ann Hall** are also buried here. See their entries that follow.

WILLIAM WIRT LOSES HIS HEAD

Congressional Cemetery is at 1801 E Street SE. The crypt is in Range 50, Site 169, or GPS 38.88117, -76.97854.

The esteemed William Wirt (1772–1834) was an advocate for arts and sciences, a brilliant author, a skilled orator, a Virginia legislator, the prosecutor of accused traitor Aaron Burr, the longest-serving US attorney general, and a candidate for president. So it's hardly a mystery why someone would steal his head, right?

After his stellar career in public service, Wirt died in Baltimore in 1934 from erysipelas, a skin infection also known as St. Anthony's Fire. He was buried in a crypt beneath a grand spire in Congressional Cemetery, where his life and legacy slowly seeped into history.

Then in 2003, William Wirt gained new life, sort of. That's when a collector named Robert L. White, a cleaning supplies salesman from Catonsville, Maryland, died. Among the bizarre mementoes he kept in his mom's basement was a skull with "Hon. Wm. Wirt" painted on it. A tin box containing the skull fell into a friend's hands, and then into the lap of Washington City Councilman Jim Graham, who finally succeeded in getting Congressional Cemetery to peek inside Wirt's crypt to see if his head was missing.

Smithsonian forensic anthropologist Doug Owsley crawled into the crypt and studied the eight corpses inside (including the body of a newborn baby that wasn't even supposed to be there). Owsley confirmed the skull was indeed Wirt's by comparing identical plant and dirt particles on the rest of his bones.

Who stole William Wirt's head and why? Nobody knows. But the skull was finally reunited with Wirt's skeleton in 2005.

*In the 1970s, someone broke into former
Attorney General William Wirt's crypt and stole
his skull.*

WASHINGTON MADAM'S GRAVE

Congressional Cemetery is at 1801 E Street SE. The grave is in Range 11, Site 92, or GPS 38.88196, -76.97682.

Prostitution wasn't technically a crime in nineteenth century Washington, which might explain why the city had more than five hundred brothels and five thousand registered prostitutes during the Civil War.

Washington's most renowned madam, Mary Ann Hall, lies beneath an elaborate marker at Congressional Cemetery.

And the best little whorehouse in Washington was Mary Ann Hall's three-story brick bordello at 349 Maryland Avenue, a stone's throw from Capitol Hill (and now covered by the Smithsonian Institution's National Museum of the American Indian, Fourth Street and Independence Avenue SW on the National Mall). According to Civil War–era maps, Hall's front porch would have sat roughly at GPS 38.887959, -77.017062.

In the parlance of the day, Hall's house was an "upper ten" establishment, meaning it stood head and shoulders (and breasts and thighs) above lesser brothels. It flourished for four decades.

Hall's bawdy house was in "Louse Alley," a seedy street on the edge of a neighborhood known as Murder Bay or "Hooker's Division," named for General Joe Hooker, whose troops camped on the future National Mall and kept local prostitutes (yes, that's why they started being called "hookers") busy.

An archaeological dig before the National Museum of the American Indian was built scoured the brothel's lot and found life there was slightly more elegant than in the rest of the neighborhood. Diggers found expensive tableware and bits of fine china, plus evidence that Hall's eighteen or so "inmates" enjoyed a healthy diet of beef, poultry, fish, and fruits, even coconuts and turtle meat. They also found dozens of champagne corks and bottles.

Hall retired from the sporting life but rented part of her property to the Washington Dispensary, which opened a women's health clinic.

Subsequent research found that after Hall died in 1886 at age seventy-one, her old brothel contained an array of elegant Victorian furnishings, including posh Brussels carpets, marble clocks, oil paintings, an ice box . . . and "elegant bedsteads, complete with feather bolsters, shuck mattresses, comforters, sheets, blankets, and pillows."

Mary Ann Hall's obituary in the *Evening Star* praised her "heart ever open to appeals of distress."

Beloved for her discretion, Hall was buried among many members of Washington's elite in Congressional Cemetery beneath an elaborate marble carving of a woman mourning over an urn. Her mother and two sisters are buried beside her.

See also "J. Edgar Hoover" (Washington, D.C.).

THE REAL NCIS

Headquarters are at 716 Sicard Street SE in the Washington Navy Yard. Access to the base is restricted; no tours are given. GPS 38.873088, -76.99613.

Since long before the popular TV franchise that bears its name, the Naval Criminal Investigative Service has been chasing bad guys and gathering crucial intelligence for the US Navy and Marine Corps.

Established in 1882 as the Office of Naval Intelligence (ONI), its main mission was collecting data about foreign navies' ships and weapons. By World War I, its agents were sent out to spy on (and occasionally sabotage) our enemies overseas, and its counterespionage role continued into the 1930s.

In 1937, ONI hired its first civilian investigator (no, not Jethro Gibbs), and by the end of World War II, it was largely a civilian agency, and criminal investigations within the US Navy were added to its intelligence role. Its mission and its name evolved over the next sixty years.

In 1966, ONI became the Naval Investigative Service (NIS) and had more than five hundred agents. In 1986, it was the Naval Security and Investigative Command (NSIC). In 1988, it was the Naval Investigative Service Command (NISCOM) and in 1992 was finally given its current name and now-familiar acronym: NCIS.

Besides its criminal investigations within the Navy, the modern NCIS has played a crucial role in Middle East counterterrorism, investigated and prosecuted Somali pirates, and become a key global player in cyber-security measures. It has its own laboratories and helps train other agents worldwide.

Oh, and the Army and Air Force have equivalent crime-busting agencies (but no TV shows). The US Army's Criminal Investigation Command is based at 6010 Sixth Street in Fort Belvoir, Virginia, at GPS 38.7025, -77.146944. The Air Force's Office of Special Investigations (OSI) is at 1535 Command Drive at Andrews AFB in Maryland, GPS 38.81334, -76.891186. As with NCIS, these agencies are on military bases where civilian access is restricted; no tours are available.

Many other major law enforcement and intelligence agencies are headquartered in the Washington area. Some are highly secure facilities that are not open to visitors; others have tours or museums, so check each agency's rules before you go. They include:

- **Department of Homeland Security,** 3801 Nebraska Avenue SW (GPS 38.938056, -77.082222). Established in the wake of the 9/11 terror attacks, DHS comprises many missions, including counterterrorism, border security, disaster preparedness, immigration, and cybersecurity.

- **Department of Justice,** 950 Pennsylvania Avenue NW (GPS 38.893678, -77.02432). This is the nation's legal arm. Under the direction of the US attorney general, it enforces federal laws, investigates crime, runs federal prisons, and pursues justice in criminal and civil matters. Among the agencies it oversees are the FBI, DEA, BATF, the US Marshals Service, the Bureau of Prisons, and all US attorneys.

- **Transportation Safety Administration (TSA),** 601 South 12th Street in Arlington, Virginia (GPS 38.863056, -77.057778). Another layer of security created after 9/11, the TSA guards the nation's air, road, rail, sea, and pipeline transportation. You've probably gotten cozy with a few TSA agents at the airport.

- **Drug Enforcement Administration (DEA),** 600 Army-Navy Drive in Arlington, Virginia (GPS 38.864426, -77.058173). Created in 1973, DEA today has 5,235 agents and eighty-seven foreign offices in sixty-three countries, all aimed at stopping illegal drug trafficking.

- **Bureau of Alcohol, Tobacco, Firearms and Explosives (BATF),** 99 New York Avenue NE (GPS 38.907468, -77.003748). When the federal government began taxing booze in 1789, antitax grumbling began and has never stopped. By 1862, the feds needed somebody to collect those taxes and prevent scofflaws, so they created a Treasury bureau whose agents became known in the sticks as "revenooers." The famed "Untouchable" detective Elliot Ness was one of them, and it was a Treasury tax-evasion investigation that finally put mobster Al Capone behind bars. The bureau morphed into today's BATF, which no longer collects taxes but investigates "booze, bombs, and bullets"—illegal gun and explosive trafficking, arson, terror, and illicit diversions of tobacco and liquor products.

- **US Marshals Service,** 1750 Crystal Drive in Arlington (GPS 38.858869, -77.049758). Established in 1789 as the police arm of the federal courts, US marshals have not only functioned as lawmen, but also as protectors of judges, jurors, and witnesses. Among the most famous US marshals are Wyatt Earp (and brothers Morgan and Virgil), Bat Masterson, Wild Bill Hickok, Frederick Douglass, and Bill Tilghman.

- **Border Patrol,** 1300 Pennsylvania Avenue NW (GPS 38.895122, -77.029996). This includes America's border guards and customs officers.

- **Mint Police,** 801 Ninth Street NW (GPS 38.900363, -77.023795). One of the oldest federal law agencies, Mint policemen must protect over $100 billion in cash, coins, and other assets stored in places like Fort Knox, Kentucky, and our national mints. Why? Because that's where the money is.

- **US Capitol Police,** 119 D Street NE (GPS 38.894668, -77.004676). In 1828, shortly after an assailant attacked the son of President John Quincy Adams, Congress established a police force to protect the Capitol and all congressmen. Lest you think the job is a cushy one, two Capitol police-men have been killed in the line of duty. (See "Heroic Capitol Policemen" in the Arlington National Cemetery chapter.)

- **Secret Service,** 950 H Street NW (GPS 38.899657, -77.0252). Founded shortly after President Lincoln's assassination in 1865, the Secret Service is charged with protecting Ameri-can leaders and important foreign visitors but maintains its original mission as an anti-counterfeiting force.

- **Central Intelligence Agency (CIA)** is at GPS 38.951944, -77.145833 in a rural area in McLean, Virginia, an unincor-porated community. It provides national security intelli-gence for policy-makers and is so secret it doesn't even have a street address. Can you visit? Ha. But the CIA's website (www.cia.gov) offers a virtual tour.

- **Metropolitan Police,** 300 Indiana Avenue NW (GPS 38.8945, -77.016561). The police department for Washington, D.C., was founded in 1861 and today has more than 3,800 sworn officers.

- **Federal Bureau of Investigation (FBI),** main headquarters are in the J. Edgar Hoover Building, 935 Pennsylvania Avenue NW (GPS 38.894368, -77.024369). The FBI was officially established in 1921 under the leadership of J. Edgar Hoover (see his entry in this chapter) as the nation's top crime-fighting force. Today, it employs 35,525 people, including 13,847 special agents who investigate terrorism and major domestic crimes, protect civil rights, fight organized crime worldwide, and do counterintelligence work. The FBI no longer offers headquarters tours, but many of its most fascinating artifacts are now displayed at Washington's Newseum, 555 Pennsylvania Avenue NW (GPS 38.892778, -77.019444). Open daily; admission charged.

  FBI and DEA recruits are trained at a sprawling compound, which occupies 385 wooded acres on a Marine Corps base in Quantico, Virginia (GPS 38.530204, -77.446318). This highly secured area is not open to the public.

  The Quantico complex is also home to the FBI's Behavioral Science Unit, which began in the early 1970s to peer into the brains of criminals as a way to anticipate and prevent violent crime, identify perpetrators, and offer more tools to law enforcement agencies. It's not open to the public, either, but credentialed researchers can get appointment-only access to the FBI's Evil Minds Research Museum in the basement of the BSU. It contains thousands of items, documents, and photos, including correspondence with some of the worst serial killers of our time. In fact, it was in the BSU that the term "serial killer" was first coined in the early 1970s.

A DEADLY DUEL 22222

Decatur House is at 1610 H Street NW, or GPS 38.900102, -77.038309. This museum is open Monday through Saturday 10 a.m. to 5 p.m.; Sunday noon to 4 p.m. Admission charged; www.decaturhouse.org.

Dueling was considered a gentleman's way of settling serious disputes in early nineteenth century America. After all, why file a lawsuit when you could take a potshot at your foe? A few cities had ordinances against dueling, but that didn't stop it. Few duelists were punished. George Washington and Ben Franklin both opposed it as a murderous practice.

In 1820, beloved American naval hero Commodore Stephen Decatur was challenged to a duel by Commodore James Barron, who claimed Decatur had insulted his military judgment after an embarrassing loss to the British fleet—for which Barron was court-martialed.

The Bladensburg Dueling Grounds were a favorite place for Washington's gentlemen to settle their disputes.

On the morning of March 22, 1820, Decatur and Barron met on the Bladensburg dueling grounds in Colmar Manor, Maryland (at the modern intersection of Maryland Route 450 and 38th Avenue, at GPS 38.93405, -76.9524). Both men fired their pistols from a distance of twenty-four feet. Decatur intentionally wounded Barron in the leg, but Barron's shot plugged Decatur's belly, and he fell mortally wounded.

Decatur was carried to his home, where he died later that night at age forty-one. More than 10,000 people attended his funeral, including President James Monroe. Decatur (1779–1820) was buried in St. Peter's Episcopal Cemetery in Philadelphia.

No charges were ever filed against Barron, but dueling was on the decline. In 1847, after one congressman killed another in a duel over a political insult (also at the Bladensburg Dueling Grounds), Congress outlawed dueling in Washington.

Commodore Stephen Decatur

PRESIDENT GARFIELD ASSASSINATED

The Baltimore and Potomac Railroad Station where Garfield was mortally wounded (now site of the National Gallery of Art) was on the southwest corner of Sixth and B Streets/Constitution Avenue NW, or GPS 38.891908, -77.020115.

Washington was already a sweatbox at 9:30 a.m. on July 2, 1881, as new President James Garfield—in office only four months—stood in the B&P station's main lobby, waiting for a train. Suddenly, an odd, disgruntled lawyer named Charles Guiteau, who'd unsuccessfully sought an office in Garfield's administration, fired his .44-caliber pistol twice, hitting the president in the arm and back.

For three painful months, Garfield lingered. His wounds—not necessarily fatal—had become grievously infected. He died September 19.

Guiteau, who'd been locked up in **St. Elizabeth's Hospital** (1100 Alabama Avenue SE, or GPS 38.8492, -76.9896), was charged with

Garfield assassin Charles Guiteau

murder. Largely defending himself in one of the nineteenth century's most watched trials, assassins tried twice to kill Guiteau (eighty-two years before Jack Ruby). More macabre, jurors were allowed to pass around three of Garfield's bullet-pierced vertebrae, removed during his autopsy. At the end of his colorful trial, Guiteau was convicted and sentenced to death.

Some 250 people—some who paid up to $300 for a ticket—were allowed to watch Guiteau's hanging at the **old D.C. Jail** (now gone) on the southeast corner of 19th and B Streets/Independence Avenue SE (GPS 38.887361, -76.976915). And he gave quite a show.

After a lengthy statement in which he claimed he was only doing God's bidding by killing Garfield, Guiteau recited a poem he had written in his death cell, "I Am Going to the Lordy." He was still speaking as hangman Robert Strong draped a black hood over his head. His final words were, "Glory, glory, glory." He was forty.

The night before his hanging, Guiteau bequeathed his corpse to a local minister, but the government refused to release Guiteau's body, and he was never buried. Instead, he was placed in an acid barrel and reduced to bones.

Those bones (along with Garfield's vertebrae) are now stored at the **National Museum of Health and Medicine,** 6900 Georgia Avenue and Elder Street NW, or GPS 38.976389, -77.0325. The museum is open 10 a.m. to 5:30 p.m. every day except Christmas; free admission. (Part of Guiteau's brain is also on display at the Mutter Museum in Philadelphia.)

Executioner Robert Strong (d. 1895), a popular professional hangman at the D.C. Jail, is buried in an unmarked grave at Congressional Cemetery, 1801 E Street SE, in Plot R19/16, or GPS 38.88253, -76.97720).

Garfield (1831–1881) was buried in Lakeview Cemetery in Cleveland, Ohio.

CHANDRA LEVY MURDER

The spot in Rock Creek Park where the federal intern's remains were found is about eighty yards downslope from the Western Ridge Trail at GPS 38.950454, -77.051132. In the past, a small metal stake has marked the spot.

Washington crime is so entangled in politics that politicians are often presumed to be involved . . . even if they aren't.

On a sunny May Day in 2001, twenty-three-year-old Bureau of Prisons intern Chandra Levy went for a jog in Rock Creek Park, a 1,700-acre preserve near her apartment (1260 21st Street NW, #315, or GPS 38.906717, -77.046744). She never returned.

The tragic disappearance of a young woman turned into a scandalous national story when Levy was romantically linked to Congressman Gary Condit, a married California Democrat who immediately became a suspect. For months, reporters hounded Condit, who insisted he had nothing to do with Levy's disappearance—but refused to talk about an alleged love affair with his former intern. The media circus was relentless.

Then in May 2002, a hiker found Levy's scattered bones on a steep, wooded slope off a popular running trail less than four miles from her apartment.

Suddenly, investigators shifted their attention to a Salvadoran immigrant who lived nearby (1424 Somerset Place NW, or GPS 38.966756, -77.034405) and was already serving a prison sentence for attacking female joggers in the park around the time Levy disappeared. With no eyewitnesses or physical evidence to link Ingmar Guandique to Levy's corpse, they painstakingly built a solid circumstantial case after clues began to emerge.

In 2009, Guandique was charged with Levy's murder. His monthlong trial even featured testimony from Condit himself, who still denied involvement and still refused to talk about his relationship with Levy.

In 2011, Guandique was sentenced to sixty years in prison. But it was too late for Condit's reputation; he had been voted out of office even before Levy's remains were found.

SPIES LIKE US

Aldrich Ames's home is at 2512 North Randolph Street in Arlington, Virginia, or GPS 38.905951, -77.106128.

Aldrich Hazen Ames (b. 1941) was a Wisconsin kid who grew up to be a CIA agent. But in 1985, the Soviet KGB started paying him handsomely for secret information, including the names of all the CIA's spies in the USSR. Ames even recruited his wife to help.

On June 13, 1985, Ames lunched with a KGB agent at Chadwick's Pub (3205 K Street NW in Washington, or GPS 38.902707, -77.063135), where he delivered two shopping bags full of top-secret information, just a taste of what Ames would give them over the next nine years.

Ames's favorite way to signal that he had information for his KGB handlers was to scrawl a three-inch chalk mark across a mailbox on the northeast corner of 37th and R Streets NW in Washington (GPS 38.913634, -77.072614), less than a mile from the Soviet embassy. The mailbox has since been removed and is owned by the newly established Cold War Museum in Vint Hill, Virginia.

At least ten CIA agents were executed in the Soviet Union because of Ames's betrayal, and many more were arrested. The CIA knew it had a mole, and in 1993 it began to watch Ames closely. He and his wife were arrested in 1994 at the $540,000 North Randolph Street house they'd just bought with cash, among other extravagances.

Facing the death penalty, Ames plea-bargained for life in prison and a five-year sentence for his wife. He remains in federal prison.

In another major espionage case, FBI Agent Robert Hanssen was busted in 2001 for selling secrets to the Soviets over a twenty-year period in exchange for $1.4 million in cash and diamonds. He pleaded guilty and is serving a life sentence.

Hanssen's five-bedroom home in the Washington suburb of Vienna, Virginia (9414 Talisman, or GPS 38.916195, -77.272038) was his base of operations for what the Justice Department has called "possibly the worst intelligence disaster in US history." At least two Russian agents working for the CIA were executed because of Hanssen's betrayal.

MR. MAYOR IS BUSTED
The former Vista International Hotel (now the Westin Washington) is at 1400 M Street NW (on Scott Circle), or GPS 38.905506, -77.033257.

In January 1990, bombastic Washington mayor Marion Barry checked into Room 727 at the Vista Hotel and smoked some crack cocaine with his mistress. He didn't know he'd been lured into an undercover sting and was being videotaped.

Barry (who famously blurted at his arrest, "Bitch set me up!") was eventually convicted and served six months in federal prison—then returned to Washington to be elected again to the city council seat and another term as mayor. He has also run into a series of other legal difficulties, including drug possession, tax evasion, traffic arrests, and probation violations.

MARY JO KOPECHNE HOUSE
The house is at 2912 Olive Street, at GPS 38.906014, -77.058529.

Once a secretary to US Sen. Robert Kennedy, Mary Jo Kopechne was a twenty-eight-year-old political worker when she and some friends rented a row house in this quaint Washington neighborhood. In July 1969, she was excited to attend a weekend reunion of RFK campaign workers in Martha's Vineyard. Kopechne left the party before midnight with US Sen. Ted Kennedy, who'd offered her a ride to catch the night's last ferry . . . but they never arrived. Kennedy's Oldsmobile plunged off a Chappaquiddick road into a pond, trapping Kopechne inside the overturned car. Kennedy claims he tried to rescue her, gave up, returned to the party, and then went home. He didn't report the accident until the next morning when Kopechne was already dead.

Some believe Kennedy had been driving drunk and panicked, or even tried to cover up his involvement, but nothing has ever been proven. He eventually pleaded guilty to leaving the scene of an accident, his driver's license was revoked for a year . . . and his presidential ambitions were permanently stained.

Kopechne (1940–1969) was buried in her native Pennsylvania. Ted Kennedy died in 2009 and is buried beside his brothers John and Robert in Arlington National Cemetery (Section S, Site 45-B, or GPS 38.881174, -77.071396).

A STRIPPER AND A CONGRESSMAN
The approximate spot of the incident is on Maine Avenue SW near the Tidal Basin at GPS 38.887665, -77.037587.

Long before Bill Clinton came to town, another powerful Democrat from Arkansas named Wilbur Mills had his own dangerous liaisons.

In the early morning hours of October 7, 1974, US Park Police stopped the drunken Congressman Mills's car on Maine Avenue SW near the Thomas Jefferson Memorial because its headlights weren't on. From the car leaped a shapely woman, who jumped into the nearby Tidal Basin before she was caught (or rescued) by cops, who soon learned that she was a local stripper known as Fanne Foxe— a frequent companion of the married, seventy-four-year-old Mills.

Although embarrassed, Mills held his powerful position for a couple months until he again appeared with girlfriend Foxe at a

Boston strip club and lost his chairmanship of the House Ways and Means tax-writing committee. He entered rehab for alcoholism and retired in 1977. He died in 1992 in his native Arkansas.

Foxe wrote a 1975 tell-all book, *The Stripper and the Congressman,* and she eventually returned to her native Argentina.

TRIPLE MURDER AT STARBUCKS
The coffee shop is at 1810 Wisconsin Avenue NW, or GPS 38.915052, -77.067576.

When a Starbucks worker opened this shop near Georgetown at 5:15 a.m. on July 7, 1997, she found a horrifying scene: three of her fellow employees shot to death execution-style in the back room.

Months later, a tipster pointed to Carl Derek Cooper, a violent career criminal. But the investigation bogged down, and a year passed before Cooper was arrested in March 1999—and quickly confessed to the Starbucks murders among many other serious crimes. He had planned to rob the store, but in the resulting orgy of murder, he left without taking any money.

Washingtonians were outraged by Cooper's crimes, which included other murders. He was indicted in forty-seven counts of murder, armed robbery, racketeering, and more. But because the District of Columbia had no death penalty, Attorney General Janet Reno made it an option by filing a federal case against Cooper—the first death penalty prosecution in D.C. in thirty years.

But before his historic trial, thirty-year-old Cooper struck a bargain to avoid capital punishment and pleaded guilty to all counts in exchange for life in prison without the possibility of parole.

In 2000, a federal judge in D.C. tossed out a lawsuit filed by a relative of a Starbucks victim and several unrelated crime survivors against America's major firearms makers and distributors.

DEATH OF A WHITE HOUSE INSIDER

Fort Marcy Park is in an unincorporated part of Fairfax County, Virginia, at GPS 38.934167, -77.125833. The Civil War cannon where Vincent Foster's body was found is at GPS 38.934357, -77.125543.

As a boyhood friend of Bill Clinton, Vincent Foster was an eager and natural choice to be the Clintons' White House lawyer. But when a series of political gaffes showed the Clintons in unflattering light, Foster took them all to heart. Panic attacks, humiliation, and depression set in.

On July 20, 1993, Foster ate lunch in his office and left about 1 p.m. At 5:30 p.m., his body was found lying on a slope beside a Civil War cannon in Fort Marcy Park. He had shot himself in the mouth with an old revolver. A suicide note/resignation letter was found in his briefcase.

Clinton confidante Vincent Foster died near this cannon in Fort Marcy Park. Was it suicide?

Foster's death was consequential enough to send a shudder through the stock market and dominate news coverage for days. Conspiracy theorists leaped into action. In 1994, the anti-Clinton Arkansas Project surmised that the presidential couple ordered the death of Foster and others who knew incriminating facts about them.

Three years later, special prosecutor Kenneth Starr—a dogged pursuer of the Clintons—ruled Foster's death a suicide, as several other investigations already had. But the conspiracy theories continue.

BRITISH POLITICAL ACTIVIST SLAIN

The crime scene is the driveway at 3124 Q Street NW, or GPS 38.910426, -77.063243.

Alan Senitt (1978–2006) was a promising young Briton with a bright political future. He had earned a master's degree in diplomacy from the University of London, worked for a member of the House of Lords, and narrowly lost election to Parliament in 2006.

Shortly after moving to America to work on Democrat Mark Warner's presidential campaign, Senitt was walking a woman home from a date in Georgetown when they were jumped after midnight by three armed muggers in the manicured, well-to-do neighborhood. One tried to rape the young woman while the other two grabbed Senitt and slashed his throat. The men escaped in a car driven by a female accomplice, and Senitt, twenty-seven, bled to death on the sidewalk. More than one thousand people attended his London funeral.

All three muggers and their accomplice were arrested later that day. Two of the men pleaded guilty to Senitt's killing; one got thirty-seven years in prison, the other fifty-two. One of the attackers was only fifteen years old.

ASSASSINATION ARCHIVES AND RESEARCH CENTER

The center is at 1003 K Street NW, Suite 640, or GPS 38.90271, -77.026217. www.aarclibrary.org.

Founded in 1984 to "acquire, preserve and disseminate" all materials about American political assassinations, the nonprofit AARC has blossomed into the world's largest private archive on the killings of JFK, Robert Kennedy, Martin Luther King Jr., and others.

Among its holdings are more than 1,500 books about assassinations, thousands of articles and manuscripts, trial transcripts, letters, photos, films, and videos, taped interviews, and personal notes—enough to fill thirty-six four-drawer file cabinets. Members have access to hundreds of thousands of documents in CD form, most gained through dogged Freedom of Information Act requests. And much of the material—more than a million pages—is publicly available through the AARC's website. The physical archives, which have irregular hours, are open to serious researchers by appointment only.

See also Lincoln Assassination chapter, and "President Ronald Reagan Shot" in this chapter.

LEGEND OF THE BUNNY MAN

The so-called Bunny Man Bridge is on Colchester Road where it passes beneath the Southern railway tracks near Clifton, Virginia, or GPS 38.78985, -77.36225.

It's one of the most rampant and unkillable urban legends in the District and its environs: An axe-wielding killer slaughters his victims and dangles their butchered corpses from a railroad bridge. And, oh, he wears a white bunny suit.

Some of the legends dating back more than one hundred years claim the killer was an escaped mental patient who hid in the woods and survived on rabbit meat. Some say he hunts mischievous children and punishes them. Some say he attacks couples in lovers' lanes with hatchets, knives, or chainsaws. Since the 1970s, several reports of an attacker in a rabbit costume have been made, and many living citizens of Fairfax County claim to have seen Bunny Man.

Nevertheless, avid researchers and police haven't found much evidence of mysterious crimes committed by the Bunny Man over the past one hundred years. They have concluded the urban legend was designed (as most are) to scare some naughty kids and trespassers straight.

Still, local legend says that if you walk through the tunnel at midnight, Bunny Man will kill you and hang your body at the bridge entrance. So, of course, lots of people test the theory.

And the Clifton General Store (7140 Main Street, or GPS 38.780674, -77.387127) occasionally stocks some Bunny Man trinkets and T-shirts . . . just in case the murderous man-rabbit misses you.

Legend says a serial killer dressed in a bunny suit haunts this rural Virginia bridge.

MURDER AT GALLAUDET

Gallaudet University, a college for deaf students, is at 800 Florida Avenue NE. The former Cogswell Hall (now Ballard North) where the killings happened is at GPS 38.909533, -76.992306.

In September 2000, the close-knit campus at Gallaudet University—a liberal arts college established by Congress in 1864 for deaf students—was rocked by the strangling of nineteen-year-old Eric Plunkett in a freshman dorm. And nightmares hadn't yet subsided when, four months later, Benjamin Varner, also nineteen, was stabbed to death with a paring knife in the same building.

A week later, students were shocked when Joseph Mesa Jr.—a deaf student—confessed to both killings. Police say his motive was robbery, but Mesa claimed a pair of "black hands" told him in American Sign Language to kill his two friends.

At his trial, Mesa said a devil sat on his shoulder, urging him to steal money. "Need money, need money," he quoted the insistent devil as saying.

A jury threw out his insanity defense and sentenced him to life in prison without the possibility of parole. Mesa is now at the Atwater federal prison in California.

BUYING DRINKS . . . AND VOTES

The George Town Club is at 1530 Wisconsin Avenue NW, or GPS 38.909706, -77.064717.

Tongsun Park was a wealthy and charming Korean rice broker who loved to throw lavish parties, especially if the guests were powerful American politicians. So it was natural that he founded the George Town Club in 1965 (with the help of some influential members of the intelligence community) where US government officials could gather discreetly for drinks and fun—even with foreign intelligence agents seeking to buy influence.

In the early 1970s, when President Richard Nixon decided to pull US troops from South Korea, Park's network was in place. With his help, Korean agents funneled bribes to as many as 115 American congressmen, aiming to reverse Nixon's plan and to gain favor for other Korean initiatives. Bribes could be as hefty as $200,000 to the most influential politicians and were often delivered in plain envelopes.

The scandal known as Koreagate broke in 1976. Ten Democratic congressmen were implicated and most resigned, but only two were prosecuted. One was acquitted, and the other served a year in prison.

Dubbed the "Asian Gatsby," Park was never prosecuted, but he remained active in political skullduggery. In 2006, he was arrested for illegally accepting $2 million from Iraq's Saddam Hussein to arrange sweet deals with corrupt UN officials in the Oil-for-Food program. He was convicted, sentenced to five years in prison, given a $15,000 fine, and forced to forfeit $1.2 million. He was released from prison after about eighteen months and returned to South Korea.

The George Town Club survived the scandal and remains a swanky meeting place for the rich and powerful.

THE NAZIS ARE COMING!

The Blue Plains Potter's Field is entirely unmarked today in the Anacostia area. It is at GPS 38.814781, -77.010032.

On June 13, 1942, four mysterious strangers walked onto a Long Island, New York, beach. Questioned by a Coast Guardsman, they claimed to be fishermen and were allowed to go.

Four days later, four more men emerged from the sea near Jacksonville, Florida, wearing only swimsuits—and Nazi forage caps. The eight men—all Nazi infiltrators with a plan to blow up and poison Americans for Hitler—rendezvoused in Cincinnati before splitting up and blending into the landscape to carry out the operation code-named Pastorius.

Against orders, two of the men visited relatives in America, and one saboteur checked into Washington's Mayfair Hotel and snitched to the FBI's J. Edgar Hoover himself. All eight were arrested on June 17, before any damage was done.

They were jailed in the District of Columbia Jail (torn down and rebuilt on the southeast corner of 19th and B Streets/Independence Avenue SE at GPS 38.887361, -76.976915) as they awaited a military tribunal to be held in the Department of Justice (950 Pennsylvania Avenue NW, or GPS 38.893678, -77.02432). Two were given life sentences and six were executed in the D.C. Jail's electric chair on August 8, 1942.

The six executed men were secretly buried near Washington's former Home for the Aged and Infirm just outside the fence of the Blue Plains Potter's Field. Their only markers were unpainted wooden slats with the numbers 276-281, no names. Later, on a dark night, American Nazi followers of George Lincoln Rockwell mistakenly dumped a memorial marker in tribute to the six saboteurs about a half mile east of their actual graves at GPS 38.813658, -77.019562.

The two saboteurs who escaped execution were deported back to Germany after the war.

The US Supreme Court ruling that allowed the saboteurs to be tried in a military court was also used to justify the military trials for accused terrorists at Guantanamo Bay more than sixty years later.

See also the "Neo-Nazi Leader Assassinated" entry that follows.

NEO-NAZI LEADER ASSASSINATED

The Dominion Hills Shopping Center is at 6015 Wilson Boulevard in Arlington, Virginia. The assassination spot is just outside a former laundromat (now a dry cleaner) at GPS 38.873835, -77.140274.

George Lincoln Rockwell (1918–1967) majored in philosophy at Brown University, but he dropped out to become a US naval officer in World War II and Korea. Along the way, he came to oppose racial integration of the military—and even proposed a plan to repatriate blacks to Africa.

In 1959, Rockwell founded the American Nazi Party in Arlington. Its headquarters were at 928 North Randolph (now an office complex at GPS 38.881414, -77.109389). His followers lived in a farmhouse known as the "Storm Trooper Barracks" on "Hatemonger Hill" (now a public park at 6150 Wilson Boulevard, where a picnic gazebo at GPS 38.870962, -77.142895 marks the general area of the house's former location). Allied with groups such as the Ku Klux Klan, Rockwell and his neo-Nazis aggressively opposed the civil rights movement and argued long and loud for separation of the races. He also insulted Jews at every turn, denied the Holocaust, and promoted socialist doctrines as he roused American emotions.

On August 25, 1967, forty-nine-year-old Rockwell was shot by a sniper as he was leaving the Dominion Hills Shopping Center, and he died on the pavement. The sniper—an ex-follower—was later convicted and paroled after only four years.

For a long time, Rockwell's admirers repeatedly painted a swastika on the spot where he died, but it rarely happens anymore.

American Nazis wanted to bury the decorated veteran Rockwell at Arlington National Cemetery (GPS 38.883044, -77.06553), but the military refused to allow mourners wearing Nazi regalia on the cemetery grounds. When public outcry swelled, Rockwell's body was cremated and his ashes stored at the Wisconsin headquarters of the white supremacist organization, the New Order.

STEAL THIS BOOK

The Library of Congress is at 101 Independence Avenue SE, or GPS 38.888694, -77.00559.

The Library of Congress isn't exactly a crime scene in the traditional sense, but at least one federal crime has been committed there.

In 1971, antiwar radical Abbie Hoffman self-published a book titled *Steal This Book,* a bestselling $1.95 manifesto that the *New York Times* called "a Hip Boy Scout Handbook," examining Hoffman's philosophy on freedom, patriotism, and bandaging riot wounds.

Oh, sure, the Library of Congress is the world's largest library with 20 million books, but it is one short: *Steal This Book* (#72-157115) was stolen in 1971. Subsequent copies have also been stolen.

ABSCAM STING

The undercover operation happened at a private home at 4407 W Street NW, or GPS 38.919269, -77.087468.

In September 1978, the FBI set up a fake company named Abdul Enterprises to nab members of Congress who'd accept bribes to do political favors for a fictional sheik. The sting was code-named Abscam.

Agents rented the house on W Street from a *Washington Post* reporter who was unaware of the sting. For more than a year, they entertained a stream of politicians, many of whom took the bait. Some $400,000 was handed out. Incredibly, Florida Republican Richard Kelly was videotaped stuffing $25,000 in bribery cash in his pockets, then asking an undercover agent, "Does it show?"

In the end, thirty-one officials were targeted. One senator and five representatives were convicted of bribery and conspiracy. They resigned or were expelled. Five other highly placed government officials were also convicted, and several congressmen were never charged but named "unindicted conspirators."

Shortly after, the government enacted laws to make it much harder to run such stings.

WHITE HOUSE, DARK MOMENTS

The White House is at 1600 Pennsylvania Avenue, or GPS 38.89767, -77.03655.

When it comes to the White House, "crime" can be a pretty squishy term. But in the history of America's most powerful address, a handful of real crimes have been committed there.

For many years, it was common (but frowned upon) for White House visitors to actually pilfer souvenirs, often snipping pieces of draperies, upholstery, or carpets. In those days, the building was open and accessible to anyone who came to the door, including some homeless men who'd sleep on the furniture.

From the Oval Office, President Richard Nixon orchestrated the scheme that led to the Watergate break-in and Nixon's ultimate downfall. He was ultimately pardoned for his crimes by President Ford, although several conspirators served prison time. (See the "Watergate" entry in this chapter.)

More than a few crimes have happened at 1600 Pennsylvania Avenue.

In the wee hours of a February night in 1974, a twenty-year-old Army private, intent on showing his skills as a pilot, stole a helicopter and hovered over the White House for six minutes. He was slightly wounded when Secret Service agents fired at him and he was later arrested.

In 1994, a drunken ex-con stole a Cessna airplane and crashed it into the South Lawn in a midnight flight. He died.

Six weeks later, a Colorado man opened fire with a Chinese-made assault rifle and sprayed the West Wing with twenty to thirty bullets before being subdued by tourists. He claimed he was just trying to save the world from a deadly "mist" attached by an umbilical cord to a mountain-dwelling alien. President Clinton was upstairs watching TV at the time.

In 2001, shortly after President George W. Bush's inauguration, an ex-IRS auditor fired a .38-caliber handgun through the South Lawn fence and was wounded by Secret Service agents after a ten-minute standoff. He spent two years in a mental hospital.

Since 1912, there have been at least thirty unauthorized trespassers at the White House, including the 2009 "gate-crashing" of a state dinner by reality-TV wannabes Michaele and Tareq Salahi of Virginia. No charges have been filed against the Salahis.

In 2011, an Idaho man who believed he was Jesus and that President Barack Obama was the Antichrist fired two rifle shots at the White House. Nobody was hurt.

NATIONAL LAW ENFORCEMENT
OFFICERS MEMORIAL

The memorial is centered in the 400 block of F Street NW, or GPS 38.89673, -77.017564. It is open twenty-four hours every day. Free admission.

Did you know that on average, one American lawman is killed in the line of duty every fifty-three hours? Dedicated in 1991, this

CARVED ON THESE WALLS
IS THE STORY OF AMERICA
OF A CONTINUING QUEST TO PRESERVE
BOTH DEMOCRACY AND DECENCY
AND TO PROTECT A NATIONAL TREASURE
THAT WE CALL THE AMERICAN DREAM

The National Law Enforcement Officers
Memorial honors more than nineteen
thousand federal, state, and local lawmen
who have died in the line of duty.

privately funded memorial honors some nineteen thousand fallen federal, state, and local law-enforcement officers who have died in the line of duty since 1791. It consists of two 304-foot-long marble walls on which are carved the officers' names.

"ORGANIZED" CRIME (ORGANIZATIONS)

Many organizations, think tanks, and lobbies around Washington focus on crime and punishment issues. Among them are:

- **Death Penalty Information Center,** 1015 18th Street NW (GPS 38.90314, -77.041548), a nonprofit resource for data and analysis of capital punishment in the US.

- **Brady Campaign to Prevent Gun Violence,** 1225 Eye Street NW, #1100 (GPS 38.901473, -77.029368), a nonprofit advocate for laws to reduce the use of guns in crime, supported by former Reagan Press Secretary James Brady, who was disabled when he was shot by would-be assassin John Hinckley in 1981. (See the entry about President Reagan's assassination attempt in this chapter.)

- **National Institute of Justice,** 810 Seventh Street NW (GPS 38.900509, -77.02211), an agency of the Justice Department that researches crime issues to improve policy, laws, enforcement, and prosecution.

- **National Institute of Corrections,** 320 First Street NW (GPS 38.893953, -77.012379), founded after the 1971 Attica riots to focus more closely on prison issues and policies.

- **National Center for Victims of Crime,** 2000 M Street NW, Suite 480 (GPS 38.905565, -77.045226), a nonprofit group that advocates on behalf of victims.

- **National Rifle Association,** 11250 Waples Mill Road in Fairfax, Virginia (GPS 38.862778, -77.335278), a nonprofit group that advocates for legal gun rights and punishment of criminals who use guns.

- **Sentencing Project,** 1705 DeSales Street NW (GPS 38.904722, -77.038889), a nonprofit promoting reform in sentencing laws and prison alternatives.

FREEWAY PHANTOM

Two of the Phantom's six known teenage victims were found dumped beside the northbound lanes of Interstate 295 about 1,500 feet south of the Suitland Parkway, at GPS 38.859827, -77.002911.

It remains one of the District's most haunting unsolved crimes: Over a sixteen-month period in 1971–72, a serial killer strangled at least six black girls and dumped their bodies beside some of Washington's busiest freeways. At least three of the girls, aged ten to eighteen, were raped—and three shared the middle name of Denise, although they were apparently chosen at random.

The killings mobilized a huge manhunt by Metropolitan Police and the FBI, but the investigation's momentum was eventually stalled when resources were diverted by the Watergate scandal.

It started in April 1971, when thirteen-year-old Carol Spinks disappeared on a walk to a local convenience store. Her body was found six days later at this site beside I-295. Second victim Darlenia Johnson, who lived near Spinks, disappeared a few months later and was dumped just fifteen feet from where Spinks's body was discovered.

A week later, a ten-year-old girl's body was found along a Prince George's County freeway. In October, a twelve-year-old girl was dumped off Pennsylvania Avenue in Maryland. In November, an eighteen-year-old girl was found on the Baltimore-Washington Parkway. And in September 1972, a seventeen-year-old girl was found beside I-295 just south of the District line.

All six were linked forever by the circumstances. One of them even carried a message from the killer in her coat pocket which ended with a taunt, "This is tantamount to my insensititivity [*sic*] to people especially woman ... catch me if you can! Free-way Phantom."

For a time, the FBI suspected a gang known as the Green Vega Rapists, which had abducted and raped dozens of women.

But then the focus shifted to Robert Askins, a deranged rapist-killer who'd been freed from prison on a technicality and was living at 1700 M Street NE (GPS 38.905753, -76.978795). When they searched his house, they found documents related to Askins's 1938 murder trial in which the judge had also used the unusual word "tantamount." But no other evidence was found, and Askins was never charged.

In 2010, Askins died at the age of ninety-one in federal prison in Maryland, while serving a life sentence for kidnapping and rapes committed in the 1970s. Because almost all of the physical evidence was lost, DNA couldn't connect Askins to the Freeway Phantom case, which has never been closed.

ROCK CREEK CEMETERY
The cemetery is at the intersection of Rock Creek Church Road and Webster Street Northwest, or GPS 38.94459, -77.01151.

Among the notable graves in the historic Rock Creek Cemetery:

- US Ambassador **John Gordon Mein** (1913–1968) was assassinated by Guatemalan rebels, the first American ambassador ever killed in the line of duty. His grave is in Section 2, Lot 42, or GPS 38.94696, -77.01512.

- Philanthropist **Evalyn Walsh McLean** (1886–1947) believed she was helping find the Lindbergh baby when she paid a con man for information about the kidnapper. She's in the Walsh mausoleum at GPS 38.946935, -77.012757. (See the entry "Lindbergh Baby Scam Victim" in this chapter.)

- Soviet diplomat **Arkady Shevchenko** (1930–1998) was the highest ranking Soviet diplomat ever to defect to the United

States during the Cold War, and he delivered a wealth of top-secret intelligence to the CIA. Surprisingly, he died of natural causes. His grave is in Section V, Lot 255, or GPS 38.95067, -77.00932.

- Former South Vietnamese ambassador to the US **Tran Van Chuong** (1898–1986) and his royal-blooded wife Than Thi Nam Tran were strangled by their own son after he was cut out of their will. The son was declared unfit for trial and deported. The graves are in Section L, Lot 158, or GPS 38.94763, -77.01283.

- Author and evangelist **Sergei Kourdakov** (1951–1973) was a high-ranking KGB agent who'd been assigned to bust up Christian gatherings in the Soviet Union. He defected in 1971 and joined an American evangelical movement to decry anti-Christian policies in the USSR—and to share secret military intelligence. At age twenty-one, Kourdakov died from a single gunshot to the head; it was ruled a suicide, but his friends and family blamed Russian assassins. His grave is in the Russian part of the cemetery at Section V, Lot 116, or GPS 38.94993, -77.00916.

- US diplomat **Francis Edward Meloy** (1917–1976) was assassinated in Beirut by terrorists allied with Yasser Arafat's Palestine Liberation Organization. His grave is in Section 2, Lot 56, or GPS 38.94690, -77.01537.

RACE RIOTS OF 1919 AND 1968

The worst urban skirmishing in 1919 happened on U Street NW between 7th and 14th Streets, centered at about GPS 38.916944, -77.026944.

On a sweltering Saturday night in July 1919, what started as a nasty rumor among drunken sailors on weekend liberty turned into one of the deadliest race riots in American history.

Both black and white servicemen were returning from World War I to find a dismal economy and poor job prospects. The District's black soldiers were also coming home to a city where Jim Crow attitudes were taking root. And local papers' headlines screamed daily about sex crimes by a "negro fiend."

In that tinderbox, a rumor provided the spark. A black man—or so the rumor-mongers said—had been arrested for the attempted rape of a sailor's white wife, but released by cops. The gossip raged through Washington's taverns and pool halls, and soon a mob of angry whites had gathered to march on the city's black districts.

At Ninth and D Streets SW (GPS 38.884848, -77.024047), whites chased and savagely beat a black man who had simply been walking with his wife, just one of many similar attacks. Blacks responded as roving gangs in cars shot at any whites they saw.

Thus began four days of rioting in which blacks mounted a deadly counteroffensive.

Black citizens rallied along U Street NW to throw back the mob. Some snipers even grabbed rifles and scrambled to the roof of the historic Howard Theater (620 T Street NW, or GPS 38.915466, -77.021134).

At Seventh and G Streets NW (GPS 38.898401, -77.021912), police killed a black rioter who had fired six shots into a streetcar full of white passengers. At 220 G Street NW (now razed at GPS 38.898333, -77.013333), a frightened teenage girl, barricaded in her house, shot and killed police sergeant Harry Wilson.

Before a thunderous summer rainstorm began and President Woodrow Wilson mobilized two thousand soldiers to stop the rioting on July 22, ten whites and five blacks had been killed. Government inquiries were promised but never happened.

In 1968, the area around 14th and U Streets NW was again a flashpoint when news broke about the assassination of Rev. Martin Luther King Jr. Starting that night and for the next four days, black rioters brought the city to its knees. Twelve people were killed, one thousand buildings were burned, and hundreds were injured. The rioting only ended when President Lyndon Johnson mobilized 13,500 federal troops. Physical scars of those riots can still be seen in Washington today, more than forty years later.

INTERNATIONAL SPY MUSEUM

The museum is at 800 F Street NW, or GPS 38.897082, -77.023556. It is primarily open 9 a.m. to 7 p.m. daily, but hours vary by season. Admission charged; www.spymuseum.org.

This family-friendly museum is dedicated to the history of global espionage—or at least the parts of it that can be revealed without having to kill you.

It claims the world's largest collection of cloak-and-dagger exhibits, including more than six hundred artifacts, nine hundred historic photos, two hours of high-tech audiovisual programs, and interactive displays. The kiddies can even participate in fun workshops that teach them how to make disguises and spy gadgets, break secret codes, and invent cloaking devices.

In the museum's gift shop, you can buy cool spy gear such as a KGB flask, a wine-bottle umbrella, and a credit card–size survival tool.

REBEL SPY . . . UNION HUSBAND

Oak Hill Cemetery is at 3001 R Street NW. The graves are in Lot 689, or GPS 38.91299, -77.05688.

Antonia Ford (1838–1871) was an elegant Southern belle and a Confederate sympathizer in Fairfax, Virginia. Union generals passing through Fairfax found her easy to talk to and never suspected she was a spy. But in 1863, Antonia was arrested and thrown—without a trial—into Washington's hellish Old Capitol Prison (which sat on the site of today's US Supreme Court building, 1 First Street NE, or GPS 38.890633, -77.005183).

But an unlikely hero rode to her rescue. Union Major Joseph Willard had met Antonia while stationed in Fairfax, and he fell in love. After winning a transfer to Washington to be near her, Willard begged her to sign a Union loyalty oath to be released from prison, but for seven long months she refused. In the meantime, she grew sickly from the poor diet and exposure.

Finally, Antonia signed the oath and was freed. She and Willard married, settled in Washington, and had three children. But her health had been irreparably damaged, and she died at age thirty-three after just seven years of marriage to her captor. Joseph never remarried and died a recluse in 1897. They are now buried together in Oak Hill.

TEAPOT DOME IS HATCHED
The so-called Little Green House once sat at 1625 K Street NW, or GPS 38.902833, -77.037333.

Once upon a time, before the suffix "-gate" was added to every Washington scandal, the phrase "Little Green House" was synonymous with political corruption.

In the 1920s, the three-story Victorian house that once sat here was a gathering place for the cabinet members and cronies of President Warren Harding's administration known as "the Ohio Gang." Here, amid whiskey-soaked poker games and a few working girls, many nefarious schemes were born, including the biggest corruption of its time, the Teapot Dome Scandal.

Harding's Interior Secretary Albert Fall, with the help of about $400,000 in bribes, leased government oil reserves in Wyoming to private companies. In 1924, the scandal was another blow to the public trust, which had been rocked just a few years before by baseball's Black Sox scandal. It was Enron and Watergate combined. Fall was convicted, fined $100,000, and imprisoned for a year—the first American cabinet secretary ever to go to prison for misconduct in office.

The actual deals were sealed in a fifth-floor dining room at the Interior Department (now the General Services Administration on the southwest corner of 18th and F Streets NW, at GPS 38.897215, -77.041916). The wood-paneled dining room itself was destroyed by fire in 1991.

LETELIER ASSASSINATED
This modest memorial is on the southeast side of Sheridan Circle, or GPS 38.911813, -77.050467.

On September 21, 1976, former Chilean government minister Orlando Letelier and Ronni Moffitt, his American assistant at

A street-side memorial marks the spot where activist Orlando Letelier died in a car-bombing.

the Institute for Policy Studies, were killed by a car bomb under Letelier's car. Moffitt, an American political activist, was only twenty-five.

The memorial sits near the spot where the bomb exploded.

Letelier had been a member of leftist President Salvador Allende's government before he was ousted in a US-backed coup that installed dictator Augusto Pinochet. Later, it was proven that Letelier had been assassinated by Chile's secret police; several people were convicted, but none served more than ten years.

BOOTLEGGER WASHINGTON

The onetime Mayflower Club speakeasy is at 1223 Connecticut Avenue NW, or GPS 38.906566, -77.041401.

During the 1920s and early '30s, Prohibition was the law of the land. But even as Treasury agents were trying to stamp out booze across America, the illegal liquor business was thriving in Washington—and some of its best customers were the politicians who made the law.

Garrett Peck, a Washington author who leads tourists on a three-hour "Temperance Tour" of significant Prohibition-era sites, says that in 1931 alone, Treasury agents busted 1,155 speakeasies in D.C. Some experts have estimated up to three thousand clubs in Washington served illegal booze during Prohibition.

One of the most popular speakeasies in the District was the Mayflower Club, a Dupont Circle nightspot where the cocktails and gambling were strictly top shelf. The building still exists, although it hasn't been a speakeasy since the 1930s.

Another prominent club was, in fact, in the living room of a third-floor apartment in a low-rise row house on K Street NW. The building still exists today, although it is now a strip club called Archibald's Gentleman's Club (1520 K Street NW, or GPS 38.902341, -77.035582).

George Cassiday, known as "the man in the green hat," was the favorite bootlegger to Congress during Prohibition. He lived in a modest brick row house at 303 17th Street SE (GPS 38.885184, -76.980946). The World War I veteran actually set up a bootlegging operation inside what's now the Cannon House Office Building (and later in the Russell Senate Office Building). He'd sometimes boast that he spent more time there than any congressman.

Interested in the Temperance Tour? Visit Peck's site for more details: www.prohibitionhangover.com.

TERROR ATTACK ON CONGRESS

The US Capitol Building is at the intersection of East Capitol Street NE and First Street NE, or GPS 38.889804, -77.009665.

It's utterly American to grumble about myriad "crimes" committed daily in the US Capitol, but this exalted place has actually been the scene of several real crimes.

On March 1, 1954, radical Puerto Rican nationalists opened fire from a balcony in the US Capitol, spraying thirty shots onto the House floor. Five congressmen were wounded, but nobody was killed, even though about 240 members were on the floor at the time.

The fusillade was unleashed from the "Ladies Gallery," a visitors' seating area above the floor, to the right of the House speaker's rostrum in the well of the House. The shooters fired from the rail area near the corner.

Four people were arrested immediately after the attack and sentenced to seventy years in prison each after their death sentences were commuted. All had been part of a terrorist gang that tried to assassinate President Truman in 1950. In 1979, President Carter freed the shooters after just twenty-five years in prison, and they returned to Puerto Rico.

That attack sparked some calls to erect a bulletproof shield between the public and the House floor, but Congress was reluctant to wall itself from the people. Today, the Capitol building has more than one hundred security cameras and one thousand police officers—and the backs of the chairs in both the Senate and House are bulletproof.

Other crime-related sites in the Capitol Building:

- Two Capitol police officers were killed by a deranged gunman in a 1998 attack. See details about that crime under "Heroic Capitol Policemen" in the Arlington National Cemetery chapter.

- In 1887, reporter Charles Kincaid exposed an extramarital affair of Kentucky Congressman William Taulbee, a Democrat. Over the next few years, Taulbee openly threatened Kincaid, and the two often exchanged insults publicly. On February 28, 1890, the two scuffled in the Capitol and

The seat of America's laws has also been the scene of a lot of law-breaking.

were separated by House doorkeepers. Taulbee warned Kincaid he'd better arm himself—so Kincaid went home and got a gun.

Later that afternoon, the two met in a dark marble stairwell at the northeastern corner of the House wing (GPS 38.889136, -77.008549). Kincaid fired point-blank into Taulbee's face, and the bullet lodged in his brain. He died eleven days later, but a jury acquitted Kincaid on grounds of self-defense.

A bloodstain on the white marble steps where Taulbee fell is reportedly still visible today.

- On May 22, 1856, Congressman Preston Brooks of South Carolina savagely beat Senator Charles Sumner with a cane

Prostitutes may have modeled for the Capitol dome's painting, The Apotheosis of Washington.

on the floor of the US Senate (GPS 38.890596, -77.00886), all in defense of slavery. Sumner's wounds kept him out of the Senate for three years, and Brooks was convicted of assault and resigned when the House tried to punish him—then was returned to Congress by adoring voters after a special election to fill his own vacancy.

- On January 30, 1835, America's long history of presidential assassination attempts began.

  President Andrew Jackson had come to the Capitol for the funeral of a congressman, but as he was leaving the Rotunda (GPS 38.889775, -77.008903), an unemployed painter named Richard Lawrence stepped from behind a pillar and fired a flintlock pistol at the president. It misfired, so he pulled a second pistol, which also misfired.

  The pugnacious president was peeved. He attacked his failed assassin with a cane as witnesses wrestled Lawrence to the ground. Lawrence (who believed himself to be the King of the USA who had been usurped by Jackson), was found not guilty by reason of insanity and died in an asylum in 1861.

- As you stand in the Rotunda, look up. The painting you see is called *The Apotheosis of Washington,* a fresco painted in 1865 some 180 feet above the Capitol floor. Full of grand metaphors, it depicts the deification of George Washington, attended by two goddesses and thirteen maidens (representing the thirteen original states).

  So what's that have to do with crime? Greek-Italian artist Constantine Brumidi reportedly used thirteen local prostitutes as his models—the Capitol's first sex scandal!

WASHINGTON'S COLDEST CASE

The site of the former Sheridan Gate into Arlington National Cemetery is at the southernmost intersection of Custis Walk and Ord & Weitzel Drive, just north of today's main entrance. It sat at GPS 38.88493, -77.067732.

April 11, 1930, was an unbearably hot spring Friday in Washington, a record ninety-one degrees by early afternoon. The capital's offices became claustrophobic sweatboxes, and as the work week ended, many workers sought a little relief by going out for walks, hoping to catch a forgiving breeze.

Mary Baker, a shy, thirty-one-year-old clerk at the Main Navy Building, left work a little after 3 p.m. that afternoon and walked about a mile with a friend to the historic Church of the Epiphany for an hour-long afternoon Lenten service. After the service ended around 5:40 p.m., the two friends said their goodbyes on the church steps (1317 G Street NW, or GPS 38.898426, -77.030503) and Mary Baker walked off down G Street to fetch her car, parked near her office near the intersection of 18th Street and Constitution (GPS 38.892159, -77.041739).

And that was the last anyone who knew Mary Baker ever saw her alive . . . except her killer.

The next day, her half-naked body was found stuffed in a culvert beside Arlington National Cemetery's Sheridan Gate, a secondary entrance on a dark, lonely road. Her blood-spattered Ford sedan was found a half-mile down the unpatrolled road. She had been badly beaten, raped, and shot three times with a .32 revolver, then dumped in the stagnant water of the drainage ditch. Some physical evidence, including a man's kid glove, were found near the body.

As the news broke, some witnesses came forward to say they saw a man in a gray cap strike a bleeding woman in the passenger seat of a car parked in the area where Baker's car had been. Before bystanders could react—even if they had been so inclined—the man sped away with the woman.

Washingtonians were startled. The assault itself was ferocious, but Mary Baker's killer had apparently struck in broad daylight while thousands of people were on the streets, not far from the White House and other highly secured places patrolled by an army of cops.

Mary Baker's father, an Episcopal minister in tiny Oak Grove, Virginia, took her battered body home to be buried in the Oak Grove (now St. Peter's) Cemetery, one-third mile west of town on Maryland Route 1301. The grave is in Lot 18, Site 9 (GPS 38.18240, -77.003884).

Meanwhile, the quiet young clerk's murder had become big news, with stories appearing every day in the *Washington Post* and *New York Times.* Homicide detectives were stumped. A couple of black men were arrested with some of Baker's possessions, but they admitted they had stolen them from her abandoned car. A dying criminal "confessed" to the crime but was cleared. And at least nine other men were arrested as strong suspects but they, too, were released when their alibis checked out.

Three months later, a real estate salesman named Herbert Campbell took a .32 revolver to police and told them he suspected it had been stolen from his house by an itinerant house painter on the day of the killing and returned the next day. Ballistics experts determined it was the murder weapon.

Scant evidence pointed to the painter . . . but police were suddenly interested in Campbell. Under questioning, Campbell admitted he framed the painter, that he might have owned the bloody kid glove found near Mary Baker's body, as well as the gun that killed her.

Campbell was charged with murder but acquitted. He claimed he had contrived the story about the gun to get publicity for a golf course he owned.

Case closed? Not by a long shot. Later that year, a jailed killer named Harry Allard "relieved his mind" by claiming he shot Mary Baker, but again, little reliable evidence linked him to the killing. Some detectives even tried (unsuccessfully) to link the murder to

Harry Powers, the notorious serial killer known as the West Virginia Bluebeard.

Who killed Mary Baker (1898–1930)? Nobody knows. It certainly generated a number of "confessed" suspects and good theories, but the murderer has never been identified. The sensational case was revisited occasionally by newspaper reporters for many years but has been cold for decades.

Lieutenant Edward J. Kelley, the lead detective who went on to become the Metropolitan Police superintendent, died at age sixty-two in 1945, and he was always haunted by the case. He is buried in Glenwood Cemetery, 2219 Lincoln Road NW; his grave is in Section F, Lot 196, Grave 7, at GPS 38.92455, -77.00678.

MASS MURDERER'S CHILDHOOD HOME
Centreville, Virginia
Virginia Tech killer Seung-Hui Cho was raised at 14713 Truitt Farm Drive, or GPS 38.854677, -77.455177.

Friends knew South Korean immigrant Seung-Hui Cho as a quiet boy, occasionally mocked for his shyness. But on April 16, 2007, the twenty-three-year-old Cho, a senior English major at Virginia Tech in Blacksburg, erupted in America's deadliest mass shooting. Before he committed suicide as police closed in, Cho had killed thirty-two teachers and students and wounded twenty-five others, far eclipsing the 1966 Texas Tower shooting in Austin by Charles Whitman (seventeen dead).

Cho, who grew up in this three-story beige townhouse on a quiet suburban Washington cul-de-sac as the son of immigrant parents, was later determined to be an insecure, mentally unstable youth whose final act was triggered by disappointments in love and academics at the university. He is buried in Blacksburg Cemetery in Blacksburg, Virginia.

MURDER AT THE HOLOCAUST MUSEUM

The museum is at 100 Raoul Wallenberg Place SW, or GPS 38.886656, -77.032147.

James von Brunn (1921–2010) was an eighty-eight-year-old white supremacist who believed the Holocaust was an enormous hoax—and he wanted to send a message to Jews.

So about 12:40 p.m. on June 10, 2009, he double-parked his red Hyundai on the street in front of the US Holocaust Museum with a rifle, intending to kill . . . and be killed.

As von Brunn approached the main entrance on 14th Street NW, security guard Stephen Johns, who was black, opened a door for him. Von Brunn killed Johns with a point-blank shot before other guards returned fire, sending startled tourists scrambling for cover. When it was done, von Brunn had been shot in the face but was alive; Johns was dead, and another guard was wounded.

A deranged gunman bent on mass murder killed a security guard at the Holocaust Museum in 2009.

A grand jury indicted von Brunn for first-degree murder, for which he faced the death penalty. While he awaited trial, the world learned more about him from his own voluminous Internet ramblings, screeds against Jews, blacks, and government. They also learned that von Brunn had served six years in prison for walking into the Federal Reserve with a handgun and threatening to take its directors hostage.

Von Brunn died in jail before he could be tried.

JFK ASSASSINATION ARTIFACTS
The National Archives and Records Administration is at 8601 Adelphi Road in College Park, Maryland, or GPS 38.999444, -76.96. It is not open to the general public, although professional researchers can gain access. For more information, see www.archives.gov.

Slain President John F. Kennedy, buried beside his brothers Robert and Edward in Arlington National Cemetery's Section 45 (GPS 38.881533, -77.071467), might be the only reminder we need about the historic implications of assassination. Nevertheless, the federal government has stored millions of documents, photographs, films, audio recordings, and artifacts related to JFK's 1963 killing as a permanent record of the event.

The bloodstained clothing worn that day by John and Jackie Kennedy (and by Lee Harvey Oswald) is in a secure, climate-controlled room here. The first lady's pink suit was donated anonymously shortly after the assassination. But don't expect to see any of it: The Kennedy family tightly controls access to the clothing, the JFK autopsy, and X-rays. The president's bloodied suit cannot be seen by anyone until 2103.

The College Park facility also contains various bullet fragments, Oswald's rifle and revolver, the windshield of the President's limousine, Abraham Zapruder's movie camera, and Zapruder's actual film itself (although the copyright is held by the Sixth Floor Museum in Dallas).

The catafalque on which JFK's casket rested while he lay in state in the Capitol is the same one built for Lincoln's funeral and is displayed in the Capitol's visitor area (GPS 38.889804, -77.009665).

Many JFK artifacts are in private collectors' hands, but the Archives preserve some pieces elsewhere. For example, the entire contents of the Dallas hospital room where JFK died, including medical equipment and a gurney, were sold in 1973 to the federal government for $1,000 and are stored in Lenexa, Kansas.

The limousine in which JFK was killed is at the Henry Ford Museum in Dearborn, Michigan.

One macabre artifact you won't find: the casket in which JFK's body was returned from Dallas. In 1966, it was dumped at an undisclosed location in the Atlantic Ocean.

See also the Arlington National Cemetery chapter, and the "Assassination Archives and Research Center" in this chapter.

THE SEX BEAST MURDERS

The Jackson Family Cemetery is a remote graveyard in the middle of a farmer's field near 12572 Cross County Road/US 522, about 7.5 miles south of Mineral, Virginia, at GPS 37.911524, -77.891658. This is private property and inaccessible without landowner's approval.

Melvin Rees (1933–1995) wasn't just a hip, quiet, jazz piano player in Washington's 1950s club scene. He was also a sexual sadist, necrophile, and serial killer who sometimes mused openly about the moral ambiguities of murder.

Nobody knows when Rees's killings began, but in 1955, he tried unsuccessfully to abduct a Maryland woman who escaped. Charges were dropped when the woman refused to testify, and Rees's friends chalked it up to a misunderstanding.

In June 1957, Margaret Harold and her boyfriend were parked in a lovers' lane near Annapolis, Maryland, when a stranger appeared beside her car. He demanded money and cigarettes, then shot Harold point-blank in the head as her boyfriend fled to a nearby farmhouse. Before police arrived, the killer had raped Harold's corpse and left, but a search of the area found a cinder-block shed whose walls were festooned with pornographic pictures and morgue photos of dead women. The odd case went cold.

Then almost two years later, in January 1959, a Virginia family of four disappeared while on a Sunday drive. Their abandoned car was found just eight miles from their home, and a huge manhunt was mounted, but no sign of the family was found until six weeks later when the bodies of father Carroll Jackson and his toddler daughter, Janet, were found dumped in a sawdust pit near Fredericksburg, Virginia. Carroll had been beaten and shot in the head; his little daughter died of suffocation after her father's body had been thrown on top of her.

Two weeks later, the bodies of mother Mildred Jackson and five-year-old Susan were discovered in a shallow grave near Annapolis. Both had been bludgeoned and raped.

All four were laid to rest on their family farm south of Mineral, Virginia.

And once again, a case of rural murder went cold . . . until 1960, when an anonymous tipster fingered a friend named Melvin Rees, whom police quickly tied to evidence from the earlier Harold murder.

When police finally found the itinerant music man, he carried notes describing the Jackson slaughter, and Harold's boyfriend quickly identified him as her killer. Rees was first convicted of Harold's murder in Maryland, then Virginia added a death sentence for the Jackson family killing but Rees never served a day in either state's prisons. Instead, a kidnapping charge landed him in a Missouri federal prison, where he died of a blood infection in 1995 at age sixty-six. His death certificate listed his profession as "piano player."

Diagnosed as a paranoid-schizophrenic, Rees is now presumed to have raped and killed at least four other women in Maryland under similar circumstances, but he was never charged.

MURDER AND THE OCCULT

Goose Creek Burying Ground is on the west side of Lincoln Road in the tiny village of Lincoln, Virginia. The grave is on the cemetery's western edge, at GPS 39.11294, -77.69643.

Dr. Robert Schwartz (1944–2001) was a renowned DNA researcher who had worked on the first nationwide database for DNA information—a tool that ultimately changed modern crime investigation.

But on December 8, 2001, an intruder broke into Schwartz's secluded log farmhouse near Washington as he sat down to dinner and stabbed him more than forty times with a two-foot-long sword, then carved a precise "X" on the back of the dead man's neck in what appeared to be a ritualistic murder.

Within a few days, police arrested three friends of Schwartz's daughter Clara, who was obsessed with vampires, occult themes, and assassin games. One of the suspects was Kyle Hulbert, a mentally ill teen who fancied himself to be a warrior and shared Clara's fascination with self-mutilation and the supernatural dark side.

Clara Schwartz, nineteen, convinced her friends that her father was abusive because he hated her friends and the way she dressed. She told them he pulled her hair, called her names, and poisoned her food, too. Later, an ex-boyfriend even claimed that he and Clara had engaged in fantasy role-playing games where Clara's avatar "Lord Chaos" asked him to kill her father.

So while Clara was at college, Hulbert went to Schwartz's farm to confront him, then slash him to death. He used the long sword, he said, because he was haunted by Clara's suffering.

Clara was eventually convicted of masterminding the murder and got forty-eight years in prison. Hulbert pleaded guilty to first-degree murder and got life in prison. A male teen who drove the car to Schwartz's farm and later called the killing "a big oopsy" received eighteen years after pleading guilty to second-degree murder; the fourth teen—a girl—cooperated with investigators and served only a few months in jail.

WATERGATE

The Watergate Hotel office building is at 2600 Virginia NW, or GPS 38.899762, -77.05538. A plaque on the sixth floor marks the suite where the break-in happened.

That one word—Watergate—has come to symbolize a thousand misdeeds, a nation's mistrust, and epic misbehavior. It's not just part of our cultural lexicon, it's a major element of our history, folklore, and political cynicism.

And it all happened right here.

On June 16, 1972, a security guard at the Watergate Hotel discovered a piece of tape across a door lock at the National Democratic Headquarters' sixth floor office—and unwittingly set in motion the greatest political scandal in American history.

That night, five burglars in business suits and surgical gloves—and carrying wiretapping devices—were arrested after they were found hiding under a secretary's desk inside the Democratic offices. Their mission (America learned later) was to gather dirt for widespread political tricks and sabotage. Their bosses were President Nixon and his top aides—all the president's men.

At first, news media treated the Watergate break-in as a second-rate burglary of little significance. But when two young reporters from the *Washington Post*—Bob Woodward and Carl Bernstein—began to dig around, this petty crime began to look more like a scandal of historic proportions.

With the help of a secret informant known only as "Deep Throat," Woodward and Bernstein pursued the story aggressively. Their reporting won the Pulitzer Prize and was the high-water mark for American journalism as it uncovered arguably the most significant story of the twentieth century.

As the White House cover-up frayed, more than seventy people, including cabinet members and Nixon aides, were convicted of crimes. Facing impeachment, Nixon resigned and avoided indictment only by being pardoned by his successor, President Gerald Ford.

The **Watergate** itself is a hotel, office, and apartment complex in Washington's Foggy Bottom district. Opened in 1967, it is on the US Register of Historic Places simply by virtue of its role in the scandal. Today, the "-gate" suffix is routinely attached to any political scandal.

The Watergate office and hotel complex loaned its name to the 20th century's most infamous political scandal.

Nixon's attorney general John Mitchell—who was ultimately convicted for his role in the cover-up and became the first attorney general convicted of a crime—lived in a three-bedroom luxury apartment there. Other Watergate residents at the time included Nixon's campaign aide Maurice Stans and secretary Rose Mary Woods (and later, a randy Clinton intern named Monica Lewinsky).

Among other key Watergate sites:

Across the street from the Watergate is the former **Howard Johnson Motor Lodge** (2601 Virginia Avenue NW, or GPS 38.900209, -77.055431). From Room 723, Nixon's operatives listened to their bugs in the Democratic headquarters. The motel is now the Hall on Virginia Avenue, a dormitory for George Washington University students.

Security guard **Frank Wills**, whose sharp eye ultimately brought down a president, was living in a boardinghouse at 1315 22nd Street NW (GPS 38.907753, -77.048651) at the time. He received no raise for his achievement, and he died penniless in 2000. He is buried in North Augusta, South Carolina.

Richard Nixon

After the burglars' arrest, the White House was in crisis mode. Nixon's frantic advisers began to control the damage with a series of desperate schemes.

In a secret meeting at **Scenic Overlook No. 2** on the George Washington Memorial Parkway (GPS 38.921062, -77.109218), the burglars' leader James McCord was promised a presidential pardon if he'd take the fall for the botched operation. And at the **Key Bridge Marriott** (1401 Lee Highway in Arlington, or GPS 38.899315, -77.073308), a Nixon aide stored $350,000 in cash that was later used to bribe the burglars to be silent.

The *Washington Post* (1150 15th Street NW, or GPS 38.90445, -77.034706) smelled a scandal. It assigned Woodward and Bernstein to follow the story. At the time, Bernstein lived on the top floor of the **Biltmore Apartments** (1940 Biltmore NW, or GPS 38.922194, -77.046416) and Woodward rented Room 617 at the **Webster House** (1718 P Street NW, or GPS 38.90956, -77.039282).

From his apartment's balcony, Woodward would signal "Deep Throat" that he wanted to meet by putting a red flag in a flower pot. Soon after, the reporter and his secret source would meet, usually in the dark **parking garage** of an office building at 1401 Wilson Boulevard in Arlington, or GPS 38.895556, -77.073333. In 2005, a former FBI agent named Mark Felt revealed he was "Deep Throat," and he died in California in 2008 at age ninety-five.

The scandal broke wide open when a Nixon aide revealed that the president had begun secretly taping conversations and phone calls in the Oval Office (GPS 38.897381, -77.037399), the Old Executive Office Building, the Cabinet Room, and Camp David. When federal judge John Sirica ordered Nixon to release the tapes, Nixon initially refused but eventually turned them over. They not only contained "smoking gun" evidence that the president had participated in the Watergate cover-up and other abuses of power, but a suspicious eighteen-and-a-half-minute gap suggested even more nefarious activities that have never been explained.

Today, some four thousand hours of Nixon tapes are stored in the **National Archives** (8601 Adelphi Road in College Park, Maryland, or GPS 38.999444, 76.96).

Among Watergate figures who are buried in the Washington area are:

- Attorney General **John Mitchell** (1913–1988) in Arlington National Cemetery (Section 7-A, Lot 121, or GPS 38.87712, -77.07110).

- Judge **John Sirica** (1904–1992) in Gate of Heaven Cemetery, 13801 Georgia Avenue, Silver Spring, Maryland (CGIV Section, Lot 227, or GPS 39.08272, -77.07291).

- US House counsel **Sam Dash** (1925–2004) in Parklawn Memorial Park, 12800 Veirs Mill Road, Rockville, Maryland (Block 201, Lot R, or GPS 39.06274, -77.10569).

For more details about the Watergate scandal, see Woodward and Bernstein's book *All the President's Men*.

2

LINCOLN ASSASSINATION

Abraham Lincoln is long gone, a victim of the most scrutinized crime in American history. But in the twenty-first century, his ghost's vapors are part myth, part textbook, and part pop culture.

More than fourteen thousand books have been written about Lincoln. His face is on our money and at least one mountain. His name is on cities, cars, blogs, schools, great and small memorials, streets, theaters, corporations, toys, highways, websites, parks, T-shirts, and a national holiday. He's been depicted in dozens of movies, commercials, plays, and TV shows—even an episode of *Star Trek*. And his legacy is evident in the laws of a still-turbulent nation that, in the end, remains united.

His legend is entangled in the uniquely American sense of justice. Not just in his role as a leader who effectively freed an entire race from bondage, but also in his role as a crime victim who was denied an ordinary ending to an extraordinary life. So Lincoln's life and death represent, in a way, both our ability to confront injustice and our occasional inability to overcome it.

This chapter presumes the generally accepted facts: John Wilkes Booth built a gang of like-minded cohorts, who planned first to kidnap Lincoln, then to kill him. On April 14, 1865, Booth shot Lincoln while other conspirators were sent to attack other officials, then fled into the countryside where he was reportedly tracked down and killed twelve days later. Eight accomplices were arrested, convicted, and punished.

The assassination of Abraham Lincoln was not just Washington's most heinous crime, but the nation's. From the bustling city of

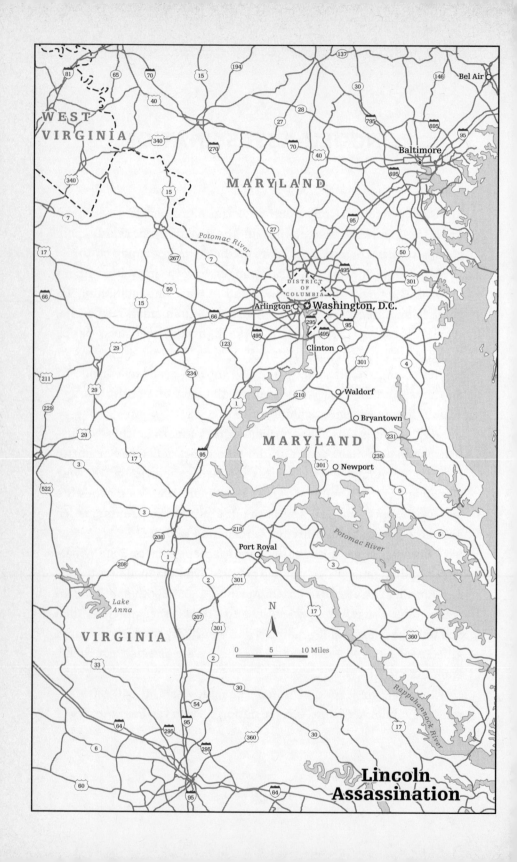

wartime Washington to the dark, mysterious woods of Virginia, this chapter lets you walk in the steps of people who changed American history for good and bad.

But it also explores the roots of Lincoln's greatness and the effect his death had on the young, struggling nation. It follows the footsteps of the assassin John Wilkes Booth and his co-conspirators as they approached their wicked task and then fled it—although none of them ultimately escaped justice (unless you believe any number of wild tales about Booth's survival into old age).

It haunts anyone who stands in Ford's Theatre, the Petersen house, or in the woods around the old Garrett farm—all crime scenes. Why? Certainly because history happened there, but also because they were the small stages on which a great crime that touches us all today was played out.

BOOTH'S CHILDHOOD HOME
Bel Air, Maryland
Tudor Hall is at 17 Tudor Lane, or GPS 39.555776, -76.302712.

This two-story, four-bedroom cottage was built in 1847 by famed actor Junius Brutus Booth, mostly as a retreat from his harried celebrity life in Baltimore (and tragically, he died before it was finished). Tucked away off Route 22 between Churchville and Fountain Green, the 3,400-square-foot Tudor Hall was the childhood home of actors Edwin and John Wilkes Booth.

Both sons followed in their famous father's footsteps and became celebrated actors, too. But before the end of the Civil War, John Wilkes Booth had become an anti-Union radical obsessed with harming President Lincoln. By the time he assassinated Lincoln in April 1865, Tudor Hall had been rented out by his family, and Booths never lived there again.

The unrestored house (now owned by Harford County) is occasionally open to visitors for very limited hours, and reservations are required. There's no admission fee, although donations are requested. For reservations, call the Center for the Arts at (443) 619-0008 or visit www.centerfortheartsharford.com.

SURRATT'S TAVERN . . . AND SAFE HOUSE
Clinton, Maryland

The former tavern—now the Surratt House Museum—is at 9118 Brandywine Road, or GPS 38.764722, -76.8975. It is open mid-January to mid-December; hours are 11 a.m. to 3 p.m. on Thursday and Friday, and noon to 4 p.m. on Saturday and Sunday. Admission charged; www.surratt.org.

In the 1850s, this part of Prince George's County, Maryland, was a hotbed of secessionist sentiment—and innkeeper John Surratt was as ardent as any. He and his wife ran this farm, post office, and tavern, which also offered sanctuary to Southern spies during the Civil War. When John died in 1862, Mary and son John took the reins of this property and John's political activism.

Struggling to keep the rural inn and farm operating, Mary Surratt decided to rent it out and open a boardinghouse at 541 (now 604) H Street in Washington (now a restaurant at GPS 38.89971, -77.020371). That's where a scheme to kidnap President Lincoln was hatched by a young actor named John Wilkes Booth and several co-conspirators. Even Surratt's son John—a Confederate courier—was recruited into the plot by Dr. Samuel Mudd.

Booth and his cohorts became regulars at Surratt's city boardinghouse, where they could safely discuss their kidnapping plan. They also used the Surratt farm to cache guns, ammunition, and other supplies.

When the kidnapping plot turned to assassination on April 14, 1865, the injured Booth fled Washington and went to the Surratts' country home to retrieve supplies stored there. He was cornered and killed at the Garrett farm in Virginia twelve days later.

The Surratts' role in the conspiracy quickly emerged. Son John (1844–1916) fled to Canada, but mother Mary was arrested, tried, and convicted as a co-conspirator. The most damning evidence against her was testimony by her farm tenant that Mary visited the tavern on the afternoon of the assassination, hiding field glasses for Booth and advising that guns be prepared for

Mary Surratt's boardinghouse on H Street became a meeting place for Booth's co-conspirators.

late-night mysterious visitors—evidence that she knew the assassination was to happen.

Less than two months after the Lincoln murder, Mary Surratt (1823–1865) was the first woman hanged by the US government (although not the first woman to be hanged *in* the US, as is often incorrectly mentioned). Son John was arrested in Egypt and returned to the US for trial, but he was never punished because the statute of limitations had passed on most charges against him.

Mary was buried in Mount Olivet Cemetery, 1300 Bladensburg Road NE in Washington. Her grave is in Section 12-F, Lot 31, or GPS 38.91072, -76.98199.

John was buried in New Cathedral Cemetery, 4300 Old Frederick Road in Baltimore. His grave is in Section J, Lot 264, or GPS 39.28806, -76.68417.

The restored tavern now offers a variety of interpretive programs about mid-nineteenth century life and the Lincoln conspiracy—and keeps alive questions of Surratt's true complicity in the plot.

BARNUM'S CITY HOTEL
Baltimore, Maryland
The hotel (now gone) was on the southwest corner of Calvert and Fayette Streets (now the Equitable Building), or GPS 39.290389, -76.612432.

In 1865, Booth's plans to kidnap or assassinate President Lincoln and top government officials were largely finalized during a secret meeting at the luxurious Barnum's City Hotel in Baltimore, where such luminaries as Charles Dickens and Davy Crockett had once stayed.

During his planning phase, Booth met with his co-conspirators in several locales, including his Room 228 at the National Hotel (now the Newseum at 555 Pennsylvania Avenue NW, or GPS 38.892898, -77.019433), the Surratt boardinghouse, and the Herndon House hotel (now gone at the southwest corner of F and Ninth Streets NW, or GPS 38.897259, -77.024119).

But Barnum's has a second connection to the Lincoln assassination: In 1869, when he was finally released after four years in prison for his controversial role in the plot, Dr. Samuel Mudd spent his first night of freedom in the swanky hotel before being reunited with his family the next day.

EIGHTH STREET "ASSASSINATOR"
Washington, DC

Congressional Cemetery is at 1801 East Street SE in Washington. David Herold is buried in his sister Elizabeth Herold's grave in Range 46, Site 44, or GPS 38.88235, -76.97838.

The son of a Navy supplier, David Herold (1842–1865) was raised in a fairly affluent home near the Navy Yard at 636 Eighth Street SE (renumbered as 1112 and now part of a larger building at 1212 Eighth Street SE), or GPS 38.877035, -76.994813. Historians have documented that Lincoln passed the Herold home eighty times and that as a young pharmacy clerk, Herold is believed to have delivered a prescription to the president.

Herold was known as a class clown and outdoorsman with a short attention span, and he preferred the company of ruffians. He didn't have particularly strong political views, but historians believe that his friend John Surratt introduced him to actor John Wilkes Booth. The promise of intrigue thrilled him.

Herold's task was to take assassin Lewis Powell (aka Paine or Payne) to the home of Secretary of State William Seward (now replaced by the US Court of Claims Building at 717 Madison Place NW, or GPS 38.899956, -77.034942) to kill Seward, then lead Powell into the Virginia countryside. But Herold lost his nerve at Seward's house and fled Washington. He met up with Booth in Maryland and stopped at the old Surratt Tavern to pick up guns and supplies before they traveled to Dr. Samuel Mudd's home near Bryantown to set Booth's broken leg.

They hid out for twelve days until they were surrounded by federal troops as they slept in a barn on the Garrett farm. Herold surrendered, and Booth was mortally wounded as the barn burned.

Making no final statement, Herold was convicted and hanged with three other conspirators on July 7, 1865. He was buried in his sister Elizabeth's grave in a family plot at Congressional Cemetery in Washington. He was twenty-three.

FORD'S THEATRE
Washington, DC

This National Historic Landmark is at 511 Tenth Street NW, or GPS 38.896654, -77.025939. It is open daily 9 a.m. to 4 p.m., except Thanksgiving and Christmas. Admission charged; www .fordstheatre.org or www.nps.gov/foth.

John Thompson Ford (1829-1894) had opened his theater barely two years before President and Mrs. Lincoln and two guests attended a performance of *Our American Cousin* there on April 14, 1865. Yet the theater already had a reputation as one of the most elegant in the nation.

At about 10:15 p.m., during the play's third act, John Wilkes Booth crept into the unguarded box behind Lincoln and shot him point-blank in the back of the head. Booth then slashed Major Henry Rathbone with a knife and leaped to the stage ten feet below. Catching his spur on a flag draped across the front of the box, he landed awkwardly and broke his left leg just above the ankle, but shouted *"Sic semper tyrannis!"* ("Thus always to tyrants!") before running into an alley behind the theater where a horse was waiting.

Army surgeons in the audience tended to the wounded Lincoln, who was removed to the Petersen house across the street. Soldiers were posted on the theater's roof as crowds began to gather almost immediately. The president died the next morning.

Ford wanted to reopen his theater after the assassination, but an angry public discouraged him. The federal government bought the building for $100,000 and turned it into an office—until 1893, when the interior floors collapsed and killed twenty-two people.

The old theater was used for storage until the 1960s when it was renovated and reopened in 1968. It is now a National Historic Landmark visited by a million people every year.

On the lower level, the theater's museum displays an extraordinary number of artifacts, including the derringer Booth used to kill Lincoln; the overcoat Lincoln wore that night; the flag that caught Booth's spur as he leaped from the presidential box; the assassin's knife, boot, compass, and spur; the inner door to the presidential box where Booth carved a peephole; the stick Booth used to jam the box's outer door closed; the chair where Mary Todd Lincoln sat that night; Dr. Samuel Mudd's medical bag; the diary Booth kept while on the run; the framed portrait of George Washington that hung in Lincoln's box; and an original wanted poster from the manhunt for Booth.

Ford's Theatre, now a National Historic Landmark, is still haunted by the memory of one deadly night.

Ford—who was initially arrested as a suspect in the Lincoln murder and spent more than a month in jail before being exonerated—went on to manage other theaters in Baltimore and Washington. He died at age sixty-four and is buried at Loudon Park Cemetery in his native Baltimore (3801 Frederick Avenue). His grave is in Section XX, Lot 234, at GPS 39.27677, -76.67780.

THE MISSING GUARD
Washington, DC

Glenwood Cemetery is at 2219 Lincoln Road NE. John F. Parker's unmarked grave is in Section Q, Lot 185, or GPS 38.92213, -77.00755.

Police officer John F. Parker (1830–1890) had been assigned by Washington's new Metropolitan Police Force to be Lincoln's bodyguard for the president's visit to Ford's Theatre on April 14, 1865. The night started badly: Parker reported for duty at the White House three hours late. When the president's entourage was safely seated in the State Box, Parker took a chair just outside the door.

But Parker couldn't hear the hilarious play, so he moved to a new seat elsewhere—then left the theater completely at intermission for a drink at Taltavull's Star Saloon (next door to the theater at GPS 38.896536, -77.02592). So Parker wasn't at his post when John Wilkes Booth entered the State Box unchallenged to shoot Lincoln. Charges against Parker for dereliction of duty were filed but eventually dropped.

Forever shamed, Parker was fired from the force three years later for sleeping on the job. He died of pneumonia and was buried in an unmarked family plot in Glenwood Cemetery.

PETERSEN HOUSE
Washington, DC

Part of the Ford's Theatre National Historic Site, the newly refurbished Petersen House (516 Tenth Street NW, or GPS 38.896758, -77.026167) is open 8:30 a.m. to 5:30 p.m. daily except Thanksgiving and Christmas. Free admission, but tickets are required; www.nps.gov/foth.

When the mortally wounded Lincoln was carried by onlookers into the street outside Ford's Theatre, a boarder at the Petersen house across the street beckoned them inside the four-story row house owned by German-born tailor William Petersen.

Lincoln died in the Petersen House
across the street from Ford's Theatre.

Doctors surrounded the dying president all night while the distraught Mary Todd Lincoln and son Robert waited breathlessly in the front parlor. In the back parlor, Secretary of War Edwin Stanton held an emergency cabinet meeting.

In a small bedroom on the first floor, Lincoln lay diagonally across the bed because he was too tall. He died at 7:22 a.m. the next morning, and his body was taken directly to the White House for an autopsy.

In 1896, the government bought the house for $30,000, and it is now maintained by the National Park Service. The actual bed where Lincoln died is owned by the Chicago Historical Society, but the bloodstained pillow and pillowcases displayed here are the actual ones used by Lincoln. Other artifacts from that long night are displayed in the Ford's Theatre museum across the street.

William Petersen (1810–1871) committed suicide in front of the Smithsonian Institution at age sixty-one. He is buried at Prospect Hill Cemetery in Washington (2201 North Capitol Street NW). His grave is at GPS 38.91864, -77.00726.

A SON'S BEDSIDE VIGIL
Arlington, Virginia
Robert Todd Lincoln's grave is at Arlington National Cemetery, Section 31, Lot 13, or GPS 38.88298, -77.06967.

Robert Todd Lincoln (1843–1926) had been invited to join his parents at Ford's Theatre on April 14, 1865, but he was too tired to attend. When word of the shooting came, Robert rushed to the Petersen house to comfort his mother, and he stood at his father's bedside when he died several hours later.

The oldest son of Abraham and Mary Todd Lincoln, Robert was the only one of four brothers to survive past his teens. After serving as a captain in the Union Army (where he witnessed Lee's surrender to Grant at Appomattox), he became a lawyer and, later, the secretary of war under President James Garfield.

Robert's tomb is a short walk from Arlington's main gate, and directly across the Potomac River from the Lincoln Memorial. From the intersection of Schley Drive and Custis Walk, it is about 130 yards southwest, atop the hill.

Read more about several eerie assassination coincidences in Robert's life in the Arlington National Cemetery chapter.

BOOTH'S ESCAPE

Booth's twelve-day flight starts in Baptist Alley directly behind Ford's Theatre (GPS 38.896713, -77.025433), where a horse was waiting for him. This alley is accessible only by a narrow entrance on F Street NW, just around the corner from the theater.

Today, you can roughly follow Booth's escape route, although the landscape is far different. Where you'll find four-lane highways,

A historic marker on US Route 301 near Port Royal marks the site of the Garrett Farm, now in the highway's median.

subdivisions, malls, and road signs, Booth found only muddy roads, far-flung farms, swamps, and shadowy figures to give him aid.

After limping offstage with a broken leg, Booth emerged from the stage door (now a metal door beneath a security light on the back wall of Ford's Theatre in Baptist Alley) and galloped away on a horse that had been held there for him by Ned Spangler. Booth was in pain.

He emerged from the alley onto F Street, where he turned right toward the Capitol and, beyond that, Navy Yard Bridge (later replaced by the 11th Street bridges at GPS 38.872679, -76.990407), then he crossed the Anacostia River into the "friendly territory" of Maryland to meet up with cohort David Herold.

Their first stop was at the former Surratt farm and tavern near Clinton (GPS 38.764722, -76.8975), where Booth had stored guns and supplies.

Assassin John Wilkes Booth

An informal sign points the way down a short path to the site of the Garrett Farm.

At about 4 a.m. after the shooting, they came to the home of Dr. Samuel Mudd (GPS 38.609551, -76.826196), who set Booth's broken leg (see a separate entry in this chapter on Mudd). By now, federal troops were in hot pursuit.

The next day, Booth and Herold sought sanctuary at Rich Hill, the home of Southern sympathizer Samuel Cox (a marker exists on the north side of Bel Alton Newtown Road at GPS 38.470346, -76.966475). They stayed at the farmhouse a few hours until Cox and rebel spymaster Thomas Austin Jones arranged to hide them for six days in a nearby pine thicket (just south of the intersection of Bel Alton and Wills Roads, at GPS 38.462967, -76.985749).

On the night of April 21, in a rowboat supplied by Jones, Booth and Herold set out to cross the Potomac into Virginia from a landing on the shore (just off Pope's Creek Road at GPS 38.397783, -76.989867).

John Wilkes Booth was buried in an unmarked grave somewhere within the Booth family plot in Baltimore's Green Mount Cemetery.

Disoriented in the dark, they paddled into Nanjemoy Creek, Maryland. They rested for a day before finally succeeding in crossing the Potomac. They asked for food at the home of sympathizer Elizabeth Quesenberry (after crossing the Potomac, turn left at first traffic light onto Potomac Drive/Route 614. The house is at the end of Potomac Drive at Ferry Dock Road, GPS 38.323168, -77.049654). But Quesenberry was suspicious and turned them away.

With a local friend as a guide, Booth and Herold continued to Cleydael, the home of sympathizer Dr. Richard Stuart (marker on Dahlgren Road at GPS 38.315983, -77.136417, and the actual house on Peppermill Road at GPS 38.31346, -77.133427). Stuart also turned them away.

The fugitives continued south to Port Royal, Virginia, where they sought refuge at the home of Randolph Peyton (at the western corner of King and Caroline Streets, or GPS 38.170467, -77.191083).

The approximate spot of Booth's death is marked with a plaque today.

But Peyton wasn't home, and his sister—believing it improper for the men to stay in a home with her—directed them to a farm south of Port Royal owned by Richard Garrett.

Two days later, federal troops surrounded a tobacco barn on the Garrett farm where Booth and Herold were resting. Herold surrendered, but Booth refused, so the soldiers set the barn on fire. During the chaos, Sergeant Boston Corbett shot Booth in the neck, and he died a few hours later on the farmhouse porch.

Today, nothing remains of the Garrett farm. A marker on the approximate spot sits in the right-of-way on US 301 about three miles south of Port Royal. The farmhouse is believed to have been in the median of modern US 301, at GPS 38.14071, -77.22837. Intrepid Booth buffs can find a small marker hidden in the trees on the approximate spot of his death. It says: LET YOUR PEACE FALL UPON THE SOUL OF JOHN WILKES BOOTH. THE TWENTY-FIRST CENTURY CONFEDERATE LEGION.

THE MYSTERY OF DR. SAMUEL MUDD
Waldorf, Maryland

Dr. Samuel Mudd's home is on Maryland Route 232 just south of Maryland Route 382, or GPS 38.609551, -76.826196. The museum is open 11a.m. to 4p.m. on Wednesday and Saturday and noon to 4p.m. on Sunday from April 1 to mid-November. Admission charged.

None of the figures in the Lincoln assassination are as enigmatic as Dr. Samuel Mudd (1833-1883). Questions have long lingered about whether he was a willing participant in the plot or a victim of circumstance.

What's known for sure is that Booth came to Charles County, Maryland, in November 1864, seeking a horse—and recruiting Confederate sympathizers for his plot. He was introduced to Dr. Mudd at St. Mary's Catholic Church near Bryantown, Maryland (13715 Notre Dame Place, or GPS 38.539404, -76.837282). Booth spent that night at the Mudd home, bought a horse from a neighbor the next morning, and then left.

A month later, Mudd met Booth and John Surratt at Washington's National Hotel (now the Newseum at 555 Pennsylvania Avenue NW, or GPS 38.892898, -77.019433), although a witness to the conversation heard nothing of a malevolent plot.

Booth and Mudd's third known meeting was historic. About 4 a.m. on April 15, 1865, a bedraggled Booth showed up with David Herold at Mudd's door, seeking sanctuary and medical help. In a

Dr. Samuel Mudd

The rural home of Dr. Mudd is a museum today.

second-floor bedroom, Mudd cut Booth's boot from his broken left leg, made a splint, and advised his friend to rest.

The next day, Mudd tried unsuccessfully to find a buggy for Herold, then learned of the president's murder—and that his guest was the assassin.

Mudd faced a difficult choice: alert federal troops to Booth's whereabouts, or go home and ask Booth to leave. By the time he returned home that day, Booth and Herold had already decided to move on.

By the time Mudd finally told federals about his visitors, it was too late. He was arrested when soldiers found Booth's boot (now displayed in the Ford's Theatre museum) in Mudd's house.

In a military tribunal, Mudd was convicted as a conspirator and sentenced to life in an island prison in Florida, where he served briefly as a doctor during a yellow fever outbreak. He was pardoned in 1869 and died at age forty-nine in 1883. He was buried at St. Mary's Catholic Church where he'd first met Booth. His grave is in the first row to the left of the church, at GPS 38.53967, -76.83732.

Was he truly guilty? Descendants have sought unsuccessfully to get posthumous exoneration for him. Presidents Jimmy Carter and Ronald Reagan both sympathized but were hampered by law from issuing pardons. All other efforts to date to clear Mudd's name have failed.

LINCOLN'S LONG FUNERAL

The East Room of the White House is at 1600 Pennsylvania Avenue, or GPS 38.897678, -77.036283.

On April 18, Lincoln lay in state in the White House's East Room all day as dignitaries and the public were allowed to view his body.

On April 20, the slain president lay in state in the Capitol Rotunda (GPS 38.889786, -77.008914) as thousands of mourners passed his five-hundred-pound casket perched on a hastily built

Lincoln lying in state

catafalque—a small wooden platform covered in black broadcloth and trimmed with silver fringe and stars. That same catafalque is displayed in the Capitol Visitor Center today and has been used for the state funerals of William McKinley, John F. Kennedy, and Ronald Reagan, among others.

On April 21, the president's casket began its long journey by train to Illinois, starting at the Baltimore and Ohio station (now Union Station, 50 Massachusetts Avenue NE, or GPS 38.897224, -77.006328). The first stop was a viewing at the Merchants Exchange Building in Baltimore (40 South Gay Street, or GPS 39.288333, -76.609444), where the public was allowed to pay its respects.

The funeral train made ten more stops over the next twelve days before arriving in Springfield, Illinois, where the president was buried in a family tomb at Oak Ridge Cemetery.

In 1922, the Lincoln Memorial was dedicated at the west end of the National Mall (GPS 38.8893, -77.050122).

TRIAL AND EXECUTION
Washington, DC

Visitors should know that the conspirators' trial and execution took place at the modern-day Fort Lesley J. McNair. As an active Army base, access is nearly impossible without prior arrangements.

Hundreds of people were arrested after the murder, but in the end, only eight were charged. The accused conspirators were first held in the Old Capitol Prison (now the site of the US Supreme Court building at 1 First Street NE, or GPS 38.890633, -77.005183). But before their trial, they were transferred to the Army's empty Old Arsenal Penitentiary, which had been converted to a storage depot during the Civil War.

President Johnson decided a military tribunal—not a civilian criminal trial—would be held on the third floor of the prison. The courtroom was in a fifty-foot section still standing as the newly restored Building 20 on Fort Lesley J. McNair (GPS 38.866929, -77.017094). A historical marker exists there at the intersection of Third Avenue and C Street.

Lincoln conspirator Mary Surratt was the first woman ever executed by the US government.

The trial began May 10, 1865, and lasted fifty-one days. The defendants were allowed to have lawyers and witnesses, but they were not allowed to testify themselves.

On June 30, the nine-member military panel reached its verdicts: All were guilty. Four (Mary Surratt, Lewis Powell, George Atzerodt, and David Herold) were to be hanged; three (Samuel Arnold, Dr. Samuel Mudd, and Michael O'Laughlen) got life at hard labor; and Ned Spangler received a six-year sentence.

On July 7, the executions took place. The conspirators' gallows location was on the site of the modern-day tennis courts (precisely, just off the playing surface of Court #4 in the far northeastern corner at GPS 38.866644, -77.017195).

After the hanging, their bodies were unceremoniously buried in four graves just south of the scaffold at GPS 38.866556, -77.017095. A crate containing Booth's corpse had already been buried in a different spot on the grounds about eighty yards northwest of the conspirators' graves (GPS 38.866898, -77.017829).

Conspirator Samuel Arnold died in 1906 after serving prison time for his role in the Lincoln kidnapping plot.

In November 1865, a fifth executed Confederate—sadistic Andersonville prison-camp commander Henry Wirz—was buried with them.

In 1867, all (including Booth) were exhumed and reburied in Warehouse 1 on the Old Arsenal grounds. With one exception, their remains were later claimed by their families to be buried elsewhere (see other entries in this chapter for locations).

Except for O'Laughlen, who died of yellow fever in prison, the other imprisoned conspirators' sentences were commuted by President Andrew Johnson after only four years.

See also "A War Criminal Is Hanged" (Washington, D.C.).

THE ASSASSIN'S GRAVE
Baltimore, Maryland

Green Mount Cemetery is at 1501 Greenmount Avenue. John Wilkes Booth's grave is unmarked at his family's request but is among many relatives in the family plot at GPS 39.30706, -76.60606.

After John Wilkes Booth fell mortally wounded at the Garrett farm, his corpse was examined, dissected, and identified. Fearing any public display of his body might erupt in rioting, it was sealed in an old musket crate on whose lid was scrawled one word: Booth. Then one night, it was secretly buried in an unconsecrated corner of the Old Arsenal penitentiary (a site inside the restricted Fort McNair at GPS 38.866898, -77.017829).

In 1869, President Andrew Johnson released Booth's body to his brother, actor Edwin Booth. The crate was exhumed from the prison yard and taken to John H. Weaver's mortuary at 22 West Fayette Street in Baltimore (now gone at GPS 39.290522, -76.615514), across the street from the stage door of the Holliday Street Theater, where Booth had often performed and which was, eerily, managed by John Ford, the founder of Ford's Theatre. There, police, friends, and family viewed the body, whose face was reportedly still recognizable, but whose skin was tightly stretched across a "grinning" skull that retained Booth's famously superb teeth. His broken left leg had become disjointed at the knee and ankle.

Under the cover of darkness on a late June night, torch-bearing mourners escorted Booth's body to his unmarked grave in the family plot in Green Mount Cemetery. His eulogy was delivered by Rev. Fleming James, an Episcopal minister visiting Baltimore from New York. When his parishioners learned of his role in Booth's funeral, he was fired.

Forever haunted by his brother's heinous act, Edwin Booth deflected questions about the assassin's unmarked grave, saying simply, "We'll let that remain as it is."

Two of Booth's co-conspirators are also buried at Green Mount. Samuel Arnold (1834–1906), who dropped out of the plot when it turned from kidnap to murder and was pardoned after four years in prison, is in Area P, Lot 40, or GPS 39.31024, -76.60609. Michael O'Laughlen (1840-1867), who died in prison, is buried in Area AA, Lot 43, or GPS 39.30782, -76.60839.

In a bizarre cemetery ritual, visitors typically leave pennies on these graves of the Lincoln plotters. Why? To remind them of the man they killed—the man whose face is on the coins.

THE BOOTH MUMMY

One might presume that the twice-buried Booth was most certainly dead and gone, but that's just not how American conspiracy theories work—even nineteenth century conspiracies.

It all began in 1870, five years after the Lincoln assassination, when a young man named John St. Helen settled in Glen Rose, Texas, where he took a job as a bartender and acted in the local theater. He reportedly had an encyclopedic knowledge of Shakespeare and remarkable stage presence. But when the daughter of a local politician invited a slew of US Army officers and a federal marshal to her fabulous wedding, St. Helen mysteriously disappeared rather than risk being recognized.

In 1871, he popped up in Granbury, just up the road. He again worked as a bartender at a local saloon (now a bakery at 137 Pearl St., or GPS 32.44211, -97.78662) and befriended a local lawyer named Finis Bates. Bates noted years later that although St. Helen was a teetotaler, he drank himself silly on one day of each year, April 14—the anniversary of Lincoln's shooting.

While in Granbury, St. Helen got sick and believed he would soon die. Secretly, he whispered to his friend Bates, "My name is not John St. Helen. I am John Wilkes Booth, assassin of Abraham Lincoln."

To be sure, he bore a resemblance to the famed actor and dastardly killer. His age (about 40) was about right, and his theatrical demeanor gave one pause. And he told a remarkable story of mistaken identity on the Virginia farm where Booth was supposedly killed by federal troops.

But St. Helen didn't die. He recovered long enough to disappear again, reportedly leaving behind a pistol wrapped in a Washington newspaper dated April 15, 1865.

That was the last anyone heard of St. Helen—until 1903, when an itinerant housepainter named David George committed suicide

The mummy of a man who claimed to be John Wilkes Booth long after the Lincoln shooting toured sideshows for decades . . . then disappeared.

in Room 4 at the Grand Hotel in Enid, Oklahoma (now a furniture store at 205 South Grand, or GPS 36.395233, -97.878297). He again confessed his "true" identity to a local widow, who described him as an intelligent man who often quoted Shakespeare when in his cups. And the coroner discovered George's left leg had been broken just above the ankle years before, and he was born in the same year as Booth. They wondered, might David George's alias be a combination of two Lincoln conspirators' names, David Herold and George Atzerodt, both hanged for their roles in the assassination plot?

George/St. Helen/Booth's corpse was mummified and displayed for two years in the front window of an Enid funeral home until his old friend Finis Bates (future grandfather of actress Kathy Bates) came to identify George as his old friend, John St. Helen. He claimed the body, had it positively identified by Booth relatives, and then launched it on a carnival sideshow tour as the mummy of John Wilkes Booth.

In 1931, a team of doctors and detectives X-rayed the mummy. They allegedly found a broken left leg and thumb, and a scar on the neck that matched wounds Booth was known to have suffered. Oddly, they also found a corroded signet ring in the mummy's stomach—bearing the initial "B." Suddenly, people began to wonder . . . could it be?

In 1937, the mummy reportedly earned more than $100,000 from midway gawkers. Various carnivals displayed the mummy over the years until it vanished completely in 1973.

Was it really Booth? Some Booth kin want to know, too. A woman believed to be the assassin's closest living relative has sought to exhume brother Edwin from his Cambridge, Massachusetts, grave to compare his DNA to samples of Booth's body now kept in the National Museum of Health and Medicine in Washington (6900 Georgia Avenue NW, or GPS 38.976044, -77.031527) and the Mutter Museum in Philadelphia.

If it matches, it's highly likely that Booth is buried in Baltimore and the mummy was just more sideshow proof that, as P. T. Barnum theorized, suckers are born every minute.

WHAT BECAME OF OTHER ASSASSINATION FIGURES?

Some key players in the drama lived out fruitful lives, and others were cut violently short.

- **George Atzerodt,** who was to kill Vice President Andrew Johnson (at Kirkwood House Hotel, 12th Street and Pennsylvania Avenue at GPS 38.882462, -76.990042) but got drunk instead, was hanged on July 7, 1865. His brother originally buried him in an unmarked grave in Glenwood Cemetery in Washington but later moved him to St. Paul's Cemetery in Baltimore (737 West Redwood), where he was buried under the fictitious name of Gottlieb Taubert. His grave is at GPS 39.288019, -76.627246. (This cemetery is open only on Saturday.)

- **Ned Spangler** was a stagehand at Ford's Theatre who might have aided Booth's escape on horseback. Sentenced to life in prison, he was pardoned after four years and eventually farmed on his friend Dr. Samuel Mudd's land. He died in 1875 at age forty-nine and is buried at the original St. Peter's Cemetery in Waldorf, Maryland (less than a half-mile from the current church at 3320 St. Peter's Drive). His grave is in the southeast corner of the cemetery, at GPS 38.61434, -76.85195.

- **Lewis Powell (aka Paine or Payne),** a Confederate soldier whose attack on Secretary of State William Seward was ultimately unsuccessful, was hanged on July 7, 1865. His body was first buried with the other executed conspirators near the scaffold at Old Arsenal Prison, but unlike the others, his body went unclaimed. Archaeologists later found a skull at the site and gave it to the Smithsonian Institution. The museum lost it for a while, then rediscovered it almost one hundred years later and identified it as Powell's. In 1994, Powell's skull was buried beside his mother at the Geneva Cemetery in Geneva, Florida.

- Rebel spymaster **Thomas Austin Jones** (1820–1895) was the Confederate Secret Service's man in Maryland. On the night of April 16, 1865, he met with Herold and the injured Booth, whom he fed and hid in a nearby pine thicket for six days. He then sold Booth a flatboat for $17 and sent the conspirators away. Jones was later arrested for his part in helping Lincoln's killer, but charges were dropped after seven weeks. In 1893, he wrote a book about that night. He later became a judge and died at age seventy-four. He was buried in St. Mary's Catholic Cemetery, 11555 St. Mary's Church Road near Newport, Maryland. His grave is obscured by a tree and a clump of daylilies at GPS 38.43548, -76.91065.

- **Corporal James Tanner** (1844–1927) lost both of his legs as a Union soldier and was assigned to be a clerk in Washington. The night of Lincoln's shooting, Secretary of War Edwin Stanton called for a stenographer to record testimony of eyewitnesses—and Tanner responded. Later, he served as the national commander of the Grand Army of the Republic veterans group and died at age eighty-three. He is buried at Arlington National Cemetery in Section 2, Site 877, or GPS 38.880027, -77.073520.

- **Lieutenant Edward P. Doherty,** credited with the capture of Booth, died at age fifty-seven in 1897. He is buried at Arlington National Cemetery in Section 1, Site 690, or GPS 38.88058, -77.07720.

- **Edwin M. Stanton,** the secretary of war who swung into action at Petersen House, died at age fifty-five in 1869—just days after being confirmed as a US Supreme Court justice. He was buried at Oak Hill Cemetery in Washington (3001 R Street). His grave is in Lot 675 at GPS 38.91275, -77.05709.

- **Frederick Aiken,** a Union officer who eloquently (but unsuccessfully) defended Mary Surratt in her conspiracy trial, died in 1878 at age forty-one while working as the city editor for the *Washington Post.* Aiken was the central character in Robert Redford's film, *The Conspirator.* His unmarked grave is in Washington's Oak Hill Cemetery in the family plot of Tennessee Senator John Eaton (Lot 79, or GPS 38.914241, -77.058550).

- **William Seward,** who was grievously wounded by Lewis Powell, died in 1872 at age seventy-one. He's buried at Fort Hill Cemetery in Auburn, New York.

- **Andrew Johnson,** who became president after the assassination, died in 1875 at age sixty-six. He's buried at the Andrew Johnson National Cemetery in Greeneville, Tennessee.

ASSASSINATION ARTIFACTS

Thousands of artifacts and mementoes of the Lincoln murder remain in collections all over the country. Some of the most valuable rest in museums and archives around the Washington metropolitan area, and many are displayed regularly. Regrettably, many more are part of private collections.

Don't get your hopes up. Not all of the artifacts in federal care are displayed regularly or at all, although some are. You might just have to comfort yourself knowing these pieces are in good, careful hands.

Some repositories, such as Ford's Theatre and the Petersen House, have already been mentioned in this chapter. Among the other local museums where assorted—and sometimes macabre—historic pieces have been collected:

- **National Museum of Health and Medicine,** 6900 Georgia Avenue NW, or GPS 38.976044, -77.031527. Open 10 a.m. to 5 p.m. daily (except Christmas). Admission charged. Tours offered; http://nmhm.washingtondc.museum.

    —The fatal .41-caliber ball that was recovered during Lincoln's autopsy

    —Some of the president's skull fragments, collected in his autopsy

    —A long metal probe used to explore Lincoln's wound and remove the deadly bullet

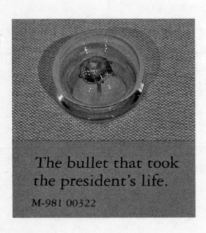

The bullet that took the president's life.

M-981 00322

The bullet that killed Lincoln

—Three of Booth's neck vertebrae, damaged by the bullet that killed him at Garrett's farm

—The bloodstained cuffs of the lab coat worn by one of the doctors who performed Lincoln's autopsy

- **Smithsonian's National Museum of American History,** on the National Mall, 14th Street and Constitution Avenue NW, or GPS 38.89088, -77.029956. Open 10 a.m. to 5:30 p.m. daily (except Christmas). Free admission; http://americanhistory .si.edu.

  —The top hat worn by Lincoln to Ford's Theatre on the fateful night

  —A military drum and drumsticks used during Lincoln's funeral parades

  —One of the canvas hoods that the seven male conspirators were forced to wear at all times during the first two months of their imprisonment

  —Detailed plaster castings of Lincoln's hands and face, made during his life

- **Library of Congress,** 101 Independence Avenue SE, or GPS 38.888689, -77.005464. Open Monday through Saturday 8:30 a.m. to 4:30 p.m. (special hours for researchers vary). Free admission; www.loc.gov.

  —The contents of Lincoln's pockets on the night he visited Ford's Theatre. These include several newspaper clippings, a couple pairs of glasses, his pocketknife, a watch fob, a linen handkerchief, and a leather wallet containing a $5 Confederate bill.

  —A playbill from *Our American Cousin,* the play the Lincolns were watching when he was shot.

The contents of Lincoln's pockets are among the items that Library visitors ask most often to see.

THE LAST WITNESS
Baltimore, Maryland

Loudon Park Cemetery is at 3620 Wilkens Avenue. Samuel Seymour's unmarked grave is in the Bethel section, Lot 441, at GPS 39.27349, -76.68484.

Samuel Seymour (1860–1956) was a five-year-old child in the audience at Ford's Theatre on that fateful night. He didn't witness the actual shooting, but he recalled years later seeing Booth leap from the presidential box to the stage. Seymour died at age ninety-six, the last surviving witness to this national tragedy.

FOR FURTHER READING

- Kauffman, Michael. *American Brutus: John Wilkes Booth and the Lincoln Conspiracies.* New York: Random House, 2004.

- Steers, Edward Jr. *Lincoln Assassination Encyclopedia.* New York: Harper Perennial, 2010.

- Swanson, James L. *Manhunt: The 12-Day Chase for Lincoln's Killer.* New York: William Morrow, 2006.

- Williams, Frank J., Craig Symonds, and Harold Holzer, eds. *The Lincoln Assassination: Crime and Punishment, Myth and Memory.* New York: Fordham University, 2010.

3

MARYLAND

AN OFFICER AND A ... CHEATER
Annapolis

Bancroft Hall, where the US Naval Academy's entire brigade of midshipmen lives, is on the academy campus at 121 Blake Road, or GPS 38.981792, -76.483523.

In 1994, some 134 midshipmen—roughly 15 percent of their graduating class—were implicated in the biggest cheating scandal in the US Naval Academy's storied history.

It all began when some middies stole a master copy of a notoriously difficult electrical engineering final exam and shared it with classmates, often for a $50 fee. Others wrote key formulas and various answers on crib sheets. And some simply lied to investigators. That might seem like common college behavior, but all were violations of the academy's rigorous honor code.

In the end, twenty-four of the midshipmen were expelled in their senior year, and sixty-two others received lesser punishment.

EDGAR ALLAN POE ... NEVERMORE
Baltimore, Maryland

Poe's grave is in Westminster Burying Ground, 519 West Fayette Street. His current grave is at GPS 39.29018, -76.62358, although his original burial site was behind the church in the same cemetery at GPS 39.28981, -76.62313.

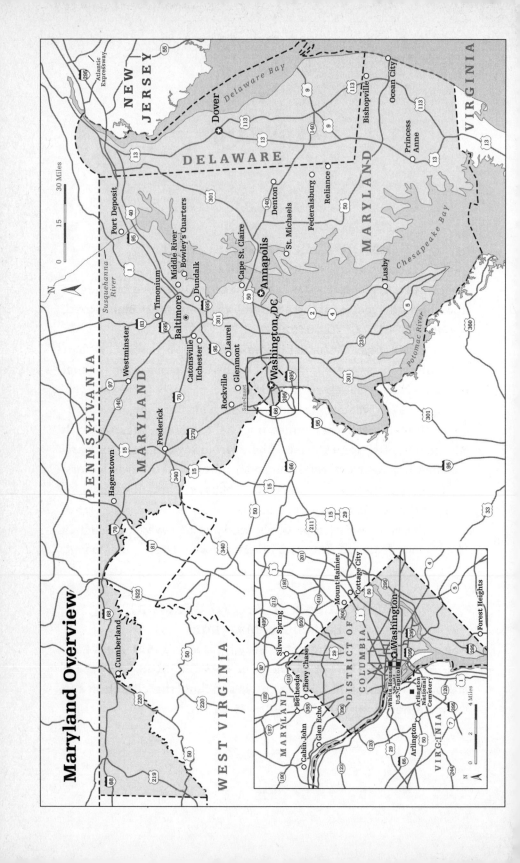

If you love mystery books, you owe a debt of gratitude (or maybe a red rose and a bottle of cognac) to Edgar Allan Poe, recognized as the father of crime fiction. His 1841 story, "Murders in the Rue Morgue," introduced the literary world to the first fictional sleuth and many of the conventions still observed by today's modern mystery writers.

But mystery also swirls around Poe's death in Baltimore in 1849 at the age of forty, launching more than a few fictional and real-life investigations.

Poe's writing life gained momentum in Baltimore in the 1830s, when he lived with his grandmother, aunt, and cousin (later wife) Virginia at 203 Amity Street, or GPS 39.291292, -76.633139. The house is now a museum dedicated to Poe's life and work.

The peripatetic Poe became famous as he moved to many homes and jobs on the East Coast but frequently returned to Baltimore as he wrote some of America's most enduring works, such as "The Pit

The author of the world's first mystery novel lies in a small Baltimore churchyard today.

and the Pendulum" and "The Tell-Tale Heart." After his beloved wife died in 1847, he grew unstable.

On October 3, 1849—Election Day—a friend found a delirious, incoherent Poe on the sidewalk outside a tavern at Gunner's Hall, 44 East Lombard Street (no longer existing at GPS 39.287833, -76.613901). Babbling and wearing someone else's clothes, Poe was taken inside the tavern briefly, then to Baltimore City and Marine Hospital (now Church Home Building) at 100 North Broadway, or GPS 39.293032, -76.594164.

Four days later, Poe died without ever regaining clarity. His death, which was subtly attributed to alcoholism, remains a mystery, but modern forensic investigators have surmised he might have been killed by epilepsy, heart disease, meningitis, syphilis, or even rabies. Others have speculated that he might have been the victim of "cooping," a form of election fraud in which reluctant dupes are forced to vote repeatedly—and to drink a lot of liquor.

Poe was originally buried in an unmarked grave in his grandfather's plot behind the church in the Westminster Burying Ground, and the unkempt site was soon overgrown with weeds and brush.

Edgar Allan Poe

But in 1875, schoolchildren, ordinary donors, and philanthropists raised enough money to build an extraordinary monument to Baltimore's literary pioneer. His body was exhumed and moved (with his aunt Maria Clemm) to a more visible corner of the cemetery. His late wife, Virginia, was moved in 1885 from her New York cemetery to be with her husband.

Also in this cemetery is a cenotaph (GPS 39.28972, -76.62336) to the memory of murder victim Philip Barton Key. His killing is described in the entry "Congressman Kills US Attorney" in the Washington, D.C., chapter.

The Poe House and Museum is open irregularly from April to early December. Hours Thursday through Saturday are noon to 3:30 p.m. Admission charged. And be forewarned: This site is in a neighborhood that can be dangerous even in daylight. It's best to call ahead: (410) 396-7932.

DRUG DEALERS STRIKE BACK
Baltimore

The Dawson family home (now the Dawson Safe Haven Community Center) is at 1401 East Preston Street, or GPS 39.305064, -76.599422.

Angela and Carnell Dawson were mad as hell that drug dealers were brazenly doing business in the blighted East Baltimore neighborhood where they were raising their five children. But in October 2002, when they asked the dealers to move elsewhere, the answer was swift and ruthless: Two Molotov cocktails were thrown through a window into their three-story row house. The Dawsons escaped unhurt with their children, but they were undeterred. They wrote a letter to police asking for help in clearing criminals from their street.

Two weeks later, a little after midnight on October 16, a bomb exploded in the house, burning Angela and her five children to death. A badly burned Carnell leaped out a window but died a few days later.

Local drug dealer and neighbor Darrell Brooks, twenty-one, pleaded guilty to the fatal fire and is serving a life sentence without parole.

The charred shell of the house was renovated in 2007 into the Dawson Safe Haven, whose mission is "to provide a safe, nurturing, caring environment for the children and parents" of the neighborhood. A small memorial garden across North Eden Street contains a few trees and plaques bearing the name of the victims (GPS 39.305045, -76.599716).

BASEBALL'S BEST BAD BOY
Baltimore

The Babe Ruth Birthplace Museum is at 216 Emory Street, or GPS 39.285556, -76.624722.

George Herman Ruth (1895–1948) was baseball's best-known and most successful juvenile delinquent, even before he became

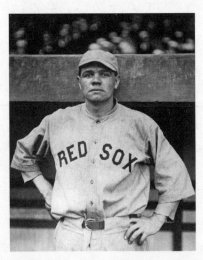

George Herman "Babe" Ruth

the most famous Yankee on Murderer's Row. He was born into a working-class family in this Baltimore row house and almost immediately began living larger than his little life. Even before he started school, he developed a healthy disrespect for authority and became street-smart in his tough neighborhood near the docks.

Babe Ruth was born February 6, 1895, at 216 Emory Street, now a museum.

He almost never attended school, hung around at his father's saloon (where he sipped booze and took up chewing tobacco), and became a petty thief—all before second grade.

By the time he was seven, his parents sent him away as an "incorrigible" to a local reformatory, St. Mary's Industrial School for Boys (which later became a Catholic high school at 3225 Wilkens Avenue in Baltimore, or GPS 39.273889, -76.670556). The tough reform school would be his home until he was eighteen, but it was there that he learned the finer points (and rewards) of baseball.

Signed by the Baltimore Orioles for $600 in 1914, Ruth emerged from a rigorous reform school to the playground of major league baseball. He proved to be a prodigy . . . and a party boy. On his way to becoming an American icon who anchored one of the best teams in baseball history as a member of the New York Yankees from 1920 to 1935 and who set baseball's single-season and career home-run records, he also lifted incorrigibility to record levels. He was a prodigious womanizer, drinker, smoker, curfew-breaker, brawler, and partier, as well as a practical joker.

Ruth lived large, and he died young. He succumbed to throat cancer in 1948 at age fifty-three. His body lay in state at Yankee Stadium for two days, and he was buried in the Gate of Heaven Cemetery in Hawthorne, New York.

The house where he was born is now a museum to his life, as well as an archive for Baltimore's professional sports teams. It is open Tuesday through Sunday, 10 a.m. to 5 p.m. Admission is charged; www.baberuthmuseum.com.

GOD EXPELLED FROM SCHOOL
Baltimore

Woodbourne Junior High School (now Baltimore IT Academy) is at 900 Woodbourne Avenue, or GPS 39.354942, -76.601956.

In 1960, when thirteen-year-old William Murray came home and told his mom that he was uncomfortable being forced to pray in his public school, she went to the school board and asked them to excuse her son from the daily exercise. The school refused.

So Madalyn Murray sued, and in 1963, the US Supreme Court upheld her complaint in an 8-1 ruling that effectively banned prayer and Bible readings in American public schools.

Madalyn Murray (later Madalyn Murray O'Hair) instantly was dubbed by *Time* magazine as "the most hated woman in America." Young William was beaten at school and received death threats. The Murray house at 1526 Winford Road (GPS 39.353213, -76.588334) was vandalized repeatedly. So the Murrays moved to Austin, Texas, where Madalyn eventually founded the American Atheists.

On August 27, 1995, O'Hair, her son Jon Garth Murray, and granddaughter Robin disappeared from their Austin home, leaving a terse note at their American Atheist headquarters. Many speculated the three had stolen the foundation's money and fled.

But six years later, a federal investigation focused on David Roland Waters, an ex-con and former office manager of American Atheists who had embezzled $54,000 during O'Hair's tenure and who fantasized about murdering O'Hair in grisly ways. In a plea deal, Waters finally admitted killing the three—plus a cohort—and led cops to the shallow grave on a Texas Hill Country ranch where he'd buried their remains (identifiable only through DNA, dental records, and O'Hair's prosthetic hip).

Waters told investigators he'd extorted $500,000 in gold coins by kidnapping the O'Hairs. He and his girlfriend spent $80,000, but the rest (ironically) was stolen from a storage locker by burglars. Waters was convicted of extortion and money laundering—not kidnapping and murder—and imprisoned for life. He died in a North Carolina federal prison of lung cancer in 2003.

O'Hair's remains were buried secretly by her only remaining son, William, the same son at the center of the landmark school-prayer controversy. Oddly, he had since become a Baptist minister.

"MONKEY TRIAL" REPORTER'S HOME
Baltimore

H. L. Mencken's home is at 1524 Hollins, or GPS 39.287501, -76.641714. Although a National Historic Landmark, it is vacant and not open to the public at this time.

Henry Louis Mencken (1880–1956) covered many stories in his long career as one of America's most esteemed journalists, but his coverage of and behind-the-scenes involvement with the infamous Scopes "Monkey Trial" was the most significant. (Mencken was the first to call it the "Monkey Trial," too.)

Acerbic Baltimore journalist H. L. Mencken, who covered some of the biggest stories of his time, lived at this Baltimore rowhouse.

In 1925, Mencken himself had encouraged his friend, super-lawyer Clarence Darrow, to defend John Scopes, a Tennessee science teacher accused of violating state law by teaching evolution in his classroom.

A caustic social critic, Mencken especially despised the American South, religion, and ignorance, and the Scopes trial gave him a platform to skewer all three. Mencken abandoned his coverage when it appeared Darrow would lose, which he did, although Scopes's conviction was overturned on a technicality, and he was never retried.

In 1948, Mencken suffered a stroke from which he never fully recovered. He died on January 29, 1956, and was buried in Baltimore's Loudon Park Cemetery, 3620 Wilkens Avenue. His grave is in Section W at GPS 39.27821, -76.67805.

Mencken's books and papers were donated to the Enoch Pratt Free Library, 400 Cathedral Street (GPS 39.294444, -76.616944). The Mencken Room is closed to the public except on Mencken Day in September (on or about Mencken's birthday, September 12) and by appointment.

Also in Loudon Park Cemetery: FBI forefather C. J. Bonaparte (later in this chapter) and Ford's Theatre witness Samuel Seymour (Lincoln Assassination chapter).

DASHIELL HAMMETT COMES OF AGE
Baltimore
The Continental Trust Building (now One Calvert Plaza) is at 201 East Baltimore Street, or GPS 39.28955, -76.612038.

Author Dashiell Hammett (1894–1961) did nothing less than elevate pulpy, gritty, private-eye prose to the level of literature. In the 1920s and '30s, he poured out short, hard-boiled detective stories for the pulp magazines and wrote five novels that became classics of detective fiction, creating unforgettable characters such as Sam Spade and the Thin Man.

Born in a farmhouse in rural southern Maryland, he was reared in the big cities of Philadelphia and Baltimore. At age twenty-one, he took a job with the Pinkerton Detective Agency's Baltimore office, housed in the soaring Continental Trust Building. It has been noted by several historians that the high-rise featured two black birds of prey—possibly falcons—over its entrance (although they're now gold-colored). Inspiration for his famous 1930 mystery *The Maltese Falcon*? Maybe.

At the time, Hammett lived at 212 North Stricker, although the house no longer exists in the area of GPS 39.291056, -76.641254. When World War I started, he enlisted in the US Army's ambulance corps, where he caught Spanish flu and later contracted tuberculosis.

Home from the war, he went back to work for Pinkerton and began writing, deftly drawing on his detective work to tell his unsentimental stories. One of his recurring and most famous characters was the never-named "Continental Op," a private-eye code-named for the Continental Trust Building where Hammett worked.

Dashiell Hammett

Over the next twenty years, he established himself as arguably the greatest mystery writer of our time, writing his last novel in 1938. He also began a thirty-year affair with playwright Lillian Hellman, one of literature's most famous romances.

When World War II broke out, Hammett enlisted again and spent most of the war editing an Army magazine in Alaska's Aleutian Islands. After the war, he devoted most of his time to left-wing political causes.

Hammett, sixty-six, died of lung cancer in 1961. Although he'd joined the American Communist Party, did prison time (cleaning toilets) for refusing to testify against suspected Communist radicals, and was blacklisted after refusing to cooperate with the House Un-American Activities Committee in 1953, the veteran of two world wars was buried with full military honors at Arlington National Cemetery (Section 12, Lot 508, or GPS 38.87666, -77.06868).

Hammett's life is described in several books, including Diane Johnson's 1983 biography, *Dashiell Hammett: A Life.*

See also Hammett's entry in the Arlington National Cemetery chapter.

THE LONESOME DEATH OF HATTIE CARROLL
Baltimore

Baltimore National Cemetery is at 5501 Frederick Avenue. Hattie Carroll's grave is in Section K, Site 40, or GPS 39.27440, -76.70782.

On February 8, 1963, the Spinsters' Ball at Baltimore's swanky Emerson Hotel (which no longer exists on the northwest corner of Calvert and Baltimore Streets, or GPS 39.289724, -76.612446) was a charity event attended by the city's swells, but "upper class" doesn't always mean "high class."

Wealthy cotton farmer William Zantzinger came dressed in a top hat, white tie, and tails, carrying a toy cane with which he delighted in whacking bellboys, coat-check girls, and anybody who came close enough.

Around 1:30 a.m., a sloshed Zantzinger wanted another cocktail and hollered at the barmaid, "Hey, black girl, bring me a drink."

"Just a minute, sir," said waitress Hattie Carroll, a fifty-one-year-old mother of eleven who had a history of high blood pressure.

But the impatient Zantzinger didn't want to wait. He called her a "nigger" and thwacked her shoulder with his plastic cane.

Later, as her shift ended, Carroll told a co-worker she felt physically ill after the confrontation, then promptly collapsed. She died soon after at a local hospital.

Zantzinger was initially charged with murder, but the medical examiner reported that the cane left no mark on her and that she had died of a brain hemorrhage likely caused by the verbal abuse, the assault, and her considerable heart problems. So the charge

After dying in a reputed act of prejudice, waitress Hattie Carroll was buried in a national cemetery.

was reduced to manslaughter, and Zantzinger was convicted. He served just six months in county jail.

Carroll was buried in her veteran husband's plot in the Baltimore National Cemetery. She was later made famous in Bob Dylan's 1964 song, "The Lonesome Death of Hattie Carroll."

Zantzinger died in 2009 at age sixty-nine. He was buried secretly somewhere in Maryland.

UNEXPLAINED DEATH . . . IN A NUTSHELL
Baltimore

The Maryland Medical Examiner's Office is at 900 West Baltimore Street, or GPS 39.288889, -76.632222.

In the early twentieth century, forensic science was primitive. Investigators weren't doctors or scientists . . . and most scientists and doctors didn't get involved in messy criminal investigations. Coroners were often just moonlighting morticians. Crime scenes were frequently contaminated by clumsy cops, curious civilians, and pushy reporters. Forensic science had not yet advanced much beyond crude fingerprinting.

But in 1931, things began to change. Frances Glessner Lee (1878–1962), an eccentric Chicago socialite who was steeped in Sherlock Holmes stories and fascinated by real-life crime investigations, donated $250,000 to establish America's first "legal medicine" department at the Harvard Medical School.

Lee's unusual contributions to forensic science didn't stop there. In the 1940s, she created eighteen scale models of genuine crime scenes, dollhouse-sized dioramas complete with working locks, tiny weapons, bullet holes (made by pin-pricks), floral wallpaper, carefully arrayed furniture, overturned dinnerware, little cigarettes, candy boxes, teeny working light bulbs, liquor bottles, bloodstains—and miniaturized victims in deathly positions. For one scene, the detail-obsessed Lee even knitted a tiny sweater by using two straight pins as knitting needles.

Each miniature scene contained all the clues an investigator needed to determine whether the death was a murder, a suicide, natural, or accidental. Calendars on the walls reflect the date of death. Magazines are scattered in some, their covers and headlines readable. The trash cans overflow. No detail is unimportant.

One scene, *The Red Bedroom*, depicts a dead prostitute on the floor of her closet. Her hands are bound with a rope, and her throat is slashed. On the floor nearby are two liquor bottles and a box of candy. Another, *The Case of the Hanging Farmer*, shows the dead man at the end of a rope over the barn beam, with his feet fallen through a wooden crate . . . and the manner of death? Accident.

Lee called her dioramas the Nutshell Studies of Unexplained Death. Twice a year, Lee herself would lead weeklong training sessions for death investigators who were forced to examine every minuscule element of the toy-sized scenes with only a flashlight

The miniature Nutshell Studies of Unexplained Death were heiress Frances Glessner Lee's contribution to forensic science. CORINNE MAY BOTZ/MONACELLI PRESS

and magnifying glass to draw their conclusions. Lee not only taught the seminars, but she laid out fancy meals for the cops on gold-leaf china, too.

After Lee died in 1962 at age eighty-three, the Maryland Medical Examiner's Office acquired the Nutshell Studies and spent $50,000 restoring them. Today, the exquisitely detailed dioramas are still used for training.

Unfortunately, they are not open to the public except by special appointment and during occasional exhibits at various US museums. But you can get an up-close look in Corinne May Botz's 2004 picture book, *The Nutshell Studies of Unexplained Death*.

GYPSY FORTUNE-TELLER BEHEADED
Baltimore

The crime scene is a two-story brick house in the 4000 block of Pulaski Highway, or GPS 39.297044, -76.563694. This is private property.

She called herself Sister Myra, a Gypsy palm-reader and fortune-teller. But in fact, Deborah Stevens was the matriarch of one of the nation's biggest Gypsy clans and often provided refuge for the caravans that followed East Coast carnivals. She was also the daughter-in-law of King Dick Stevens, an American Gypsy leader who lived in the Baltimore area until his death in 1959.

On November 16, 1994, Stevens was found decapitated in the austere brick building that served as her office, home, and "reading room."

Within hours, police had arrested Douglas Thomas Clark, twenty-eight, a frequent customer of Sister Myra's who had tried to commit suicide by leaping in front of an Amtrak train near the crime scene. Clark, who confessed that he sawed Stevens's head off because he thought she was a demon, eventually pleaded guilty but insane and was committed to a mental institution

NUN'S MURDER GOES COLD
Baltimore

The Carriage House Apartments are at 131 North Bend Road, or GPS 39.282385, -76.705337.

In November 1969, Sister Catherine Ann Cesnik (1942–1969) was coming home to her apartment from the store when she disappeared. Two months later, the well-liked twenty-six-year-old teacher's badly decomposed and vermin-eaten body was found in a snowy, vacant field. Although police couldn't tell too much from her remains, she died from blunt-force trauma, and the back of her skull bore a hole the size of a quarter.

Sister Cathy had been granted "exclaustration," permission from the church to live outside the convent under relaxed vows. She was buried at St. Mary's Cemetery in Sharpsburg, Pennsylvania.

Cops focused on the Catholic school where Sister Cathy had recently taught, Archbishop Keough High School for Girls (now Seton Keough High School), 1201 Caton Avenue (GPS 39.269167, -76.666111). At least one detective was disturbed by rumors of rampant sexual misbehavior at the school and theorized that Sister Cathy might have been planning to blow the whistle.

Investigators grilled Sister Cathy's acquaintances, including a Jesuit priest with whom she had a romantic relationship, and an allegedly abusive priest at the school.

Why? According to police, whoever killed her had parked her Ford Maverick at an odd angle near her apartment, five miles from where her body was found. What random killer carefully returns a victim's car to her neighborhood and risks being caught?

But the trail went cold, and Sister Cathy's killer has never been identified, although cold-case detectives recently took a new look at the killing, without success.

THE "ALMOST PERFECT" CRIME
Baltimore

The crash spot is on the east side of Taylor Avenue near the intersection with Belair Road, at GPS 39.361554, -76.524756.

To the two policemen who actually witnessed the crash on a September night in 1952, it all looked like a tragic accident. Shortly after midnight, a Chrysler sedan careened down the Taylor Avenue hill at about sixty miles per hour, swerved to hit a telephone pole, then sideswiped a tree and rolled over. Within seconds, the cops were pulling the driver—thirty-three-year-old mother of three, Dorothy May Grammer—from the vehicle. But it was too late. She was already dead.

Simple traffic accident, right? Not so fast. Dorothy's car didn't sustain the kind of damage that would have crushed and mangled her skull the way they found it. The cops also found a puddle of coagulated blood on the driver's seat, but blood requires a few minutes to clot, and they had arrived in seconds. More intriguing, the accelerator had been wedged down with a small stone.

The coroner ruled it a homicide. The prime suspect? Her husband.

George Edward Grammer was a manager for a New York metals firm and denied any involvement. But as the facts piled up against him in the days after the crash, he confessed that he had bludgeoned his wife with a pipe, stuffed her corpse in the family car, and staged the "accident" so he could be with his mistress. In return for his plea, the prosecutor promised a life sentence.

But Grammer miscalculated. In court, he changed his plea to "not guilty" and went back to his original tale of a tragic mishap. The judge didn't buy it, and Grammer was sentenced to death.

On June 11, 1954, he was hanged.

KATYN MASSACRE REMEMBERED
Baltimore

The memorial is in the circle of President Street where it intersects Aliceanna Street, or GPS 39.283181, -76.601604.

In 1939, the Soviet Union and Nazi Germany invaded Poland, and the Polish army quickly surrendered to the Russians, even though no declaration of war had ever been made. More than twenty thousand Polish officers and others became political prisoners. But in 1940, Stalin ordered that they all be executed.

The officers were actually murdered in three separate sites, but the Katyn Forest near Smolensk, Russia, was the main site and became a potent symbol of the massacre. Katyn's dead were buried in a mass grave in the forest, which was eventually unearthed by the Nazis in 1943 and shocked the world.

The brainchild of the local Polish community, Baltimore's Katyn Memorial was dedicated in 2000. The twelve-ton, forty-four-foot-tall sculpture by Polish-born artist Andrzej Pitynski depicts an eagle—Poland's national symbol—rising from the flames.

A NUN'S SHOCKING MURDER
Baltimore

The convent of the Franciscan Sisters of Baltimore is at 3725 Ellerslie Avenue, or GPS 39.336111, -76.603611. This is private property.

Sister MaryAnn Glinka rose at 5 a.m. on March 19, 1993, as she did every morning. She padded downstairs in her nightgown to fix breakfast for the nuns at her convent, the Franciscan Sisters of Baltimore.

But around 5:30 a.m., when the first nuns arrived for breakfast, they found Sister MaryAnn lying dead in the front hallway, her hands and feet bound. She had been raped, and her killer had stuffed a small change purse in her mouth before strangling her with the belt of her robe.

Investigators found the glass of a side door had been broken, and some rooms had been ransacked, probably by a burglar who'd been surprised by Sister MaryAnn.

But the killer had made some serious mistakes. He left behind a matchbook with his girlfriend's phone number and his fingerprints on the cellophane of an unopened box of candy.

Cops immediately focused on Melvin L. Jones, a thirty-four-year-old killer who had worked at the convent in the late 1980s as a painter. When Jones was arrested two weeks after the killing, police found Sister MaryAnn's wristwatch in his pocket. They also discovered Jones had just been paroled from a prison sentence for manslaughter and slipped through the cracks of probation offices in both North Carolina and Maryland.

Jones was convicted of first-degree murder, attempted rape, robbery, burglary, and breaking and entering. He was sentenced to life without parole.

Sister MaryAnn, fifty-one, had supervised St. Elizabeth's School and Habilitation Center for mentally handicapped black teenagers in North Baltimore. She was buried in the convent's private cemetery (GPS 39.335309, -76.602755) on the convent's wooded, thirteen-acre grounds.

THE FIRST SPYMASTER
Baltimore

Green Mount Cemetery is at 1501 Greenmount Avenue. Dulles's grave is in the McDonogh section, Lot 51, or GPS 39.30730, -76.60455.

Allen Welsh Dulles (1893–1969) was a stellar spy for the Office of Strategic Services (OSS) during World War II who became the director of the fledgling CIA in 1953. His tenure had its ups and downs—from successes like Radio Free Europe and the earliest reconnaissance satellites to failures such as the U-2 spy plane crash in the Soviet Union and the Bay of Pigs. He resigned in 1961 and later served on the Warren Commission investigating JFK's assassination.

Also in Green Mount Cemetery are the graves of Lincoln conspirators John Wilkes Booth, Samuel Arnold, and Michael O'Laughlen. See the Lincoln Assassination chapter for more details.

HOMICIDE ON THE TV
Baltimore

A plaque marks the spot of the main production and filming of TV's *Homicide: Life on the Street* at the Recreation Pier on the waterside of the 1700 block of Thames Street, or GPS 39.281667, -76.591944.

For seven seasons, from 1993 to 1999, *Homicide: Life on the Street* rocked prime-time TV. The gritty, fictional drama was based on a nonfiction book by *Baltimore Sun* writer David Simon, *Homicide: A Year on the Killing Streets,* in which he followed a Baltimore homicide unit. It starred such notable actors as Yaphet Kotto, Andre Braugher, Ned Beatty, Melissa Leo, and Richard Belzer, who eventually migrated his John Munch character to *Law & Order: SVU.*

The center of the action was the doughty brick building that served as the unit's dank headquarters. Loyal viewers will remember the dry-erase board on which the detectives tracked their cases, a real technique used by Baltimore's real homicide detectives at the time.

Want to visit some of the locations in the historic Fells Point area that appeared in the show? Right across from the "headquarters" building on Recreation Pier is the **Waterfront Hotel,** 1710 Thames Street (GPS 39.281981, -76.592141). This became a favorite watering hole for the gravely overworked detectives and was the site of the fictional bar owned by Munch.

A few other hangouts that got significant screen time were **Jimmy's Restaurant,** 801 South Broadway (GPS 39.282502, -76.592823); **The Wharf Rat,** 801 Ann Street (GPS 39.282594, -76.59106); and **The Horse You Came in On,** 1626 Thames (GPS 39.281475, -76.594093).

Most of the TV crime drama Homicide: Life on the Street *was filmed in this Baltimore neighborhood.*

FOREFATHER OF THE FBI
Baltimore

Loudon Park Cemetery is at 3620 Wilkens Avenue. The Bonaparte family plot is in Section B, Lot 37, at GPS 39.28037, -76.67932.

New York–born Charles Joseph Bonaparte (1851–1921) was the grand-nephew of Napoleon but made his own impact in American politics.

After Bonaparte graduated from Harvard Law School in 1874, he opened a practice in Baltimore and became active in rooting out political corruption, which was rife at the time. He founded a good-government organization—derided as "googoos"—in 1894 to fight bribery and influence-peddling in government.

In 1905, President Teddy Roosevelt appointed Bonaparte as Secretary of the Navy, and in 1906 the US attorney general.

As it undertook trust-busting of the tobacco monopoly, the Justice Department was hampered by a lack of its own investigation team and had to borrow Treasury and Secret Service agents. So in 1908, Bonaparte—now nicknamed "Charlie the Crook Chaser"—pulled together twenty-three "special agents" as the first investigative force within the Justice Department. In 1935, Bonaparte's team and another created in 1920 under J. Edgar Hoover merged to become the Federal Bureau of Investigation.

After leaving office in 1909, Bonaparte continued as an active civic reformer and died in 1921 at age seventy at his Baltimore-area estate known as Bella Vista (renamed Mount Vista Mansion after a fire in the 1930s).

For more about the early FBI, see "The Palmer Bombing" (Washington, D.C.). See also "'Monkey Trial' Reporter's Home" in this chapter and "The Last Witness" (Lincoln Assassination), both of which feature people buried in Loudon Park Cemetery.

DEADLY SECESSIONIST RIOTS
Baltimore

The historic President Street train station is at 601 President Street, or GPS 39.283999, -76.602345. Its Baltimore Civil War Museum is open daily 10 a.m. to 5 p.m. Admission charged.

Just a few days after the Civil War began in April 1861, Union troops destined for Washington, D.C., were passing through the city when pro-Southern citizens erupted in violence against them.

Because locomotives weren't allowed on city streets, the train cars were drawn by horses from the President Street Station down Pratt Street to the Camden Station (GPS 39.284944, -76.619457), while at least four Union companies made the trip on foot.

Along the way, pro-secessionist locals attacked the soldiers, who fought back. Four troopers and twelve civilians were killed—some of the first deaths of the war—before the Northern soldiers escaped the mob, and no charges were ever filed.

Today, you can walk the 1.6-mile route of the riot, which features several interpretive markers. Guided tours can be arranged at the President Street Station.

METROPOLITAN TRANSITION CENTER
Baltimore

This former Maryland prison and death chamber is at 954 Forest Street, or GPS 39.299167, -76.606944.

Although much smaller at the time, this urban prison was established in 1811 as the Maryland Penitentiary, only the second in the US. It quickly gained a reputation as a squalid, cruel, and corrupt place. Until 2010, it housed Maryland's Death Row, where all five condemned men to be executed here since 1976 died by lethal injection.

Today, the Metropolitan Transition Center houses only short-term offenders. Maximum-security inmates are jailed elsewhere.

PERFECT LIFE, PERFECT CRIME?
Bethesda

The house is at 8103 Lilly Stone Drive, or GPS 38.9875, -77.163056. This is private property.

Yale-educated Bradford Bishop (b. 1936) was a thirty-nine-year-old diplomat with the US State Department in 1976. A former Army intelligence officer who was fluent in five languages, Bishop lived a seemingly perfect life with his mother, his wife (and high school sweetheart), Annette, and their three young sons in this sedate suburb.

On March 1, 1976, Bishop learned that he didn't get an expected promotion. He told his secretary he felt ill and left work. On the way home, he stopped at a Sears store and bought a ball-peen hammer, a shovel, and a gas can (which he filled after he left the store).

He arrived home sometime after 8 p.m. and bludgeoned his wife with the hammer. Then he killed his sixty-eight-year-old mother and his three boys, aged five to fourteen, while they slept.

Bishop then loaded the corpses in the family station wagon and drove six hours to a secluded woodland in North Carolina, where he laid them in a shallow grave and set them ablaze. The next day, a forest ranger found the burned corpses and a shovel still bearing the label of the Sears store where Bishop bought it. The bodies were identified a week later when a neighbor discovered the blood-spattered crime scene inside Bishop's house.

On March 18, Bishop's car was found abandoned at a campground in the Great Smoky Mountains National Park. He had vanished, and he has never been found.

Is he alive or dead? Nobody knows. Bishop has reportedly been seen in several overseas locations, but he has never been caught. With his intelligence training and experience at embassies in Italy, Ethiopia, and Botswana, he could easily have melted forever into a foreign population. No unidentified bodies found on the Eastern Seaboard since 1976 match him. A warrant for Bishop's arrest remains active.

MASS MURDER ON THE EASTERN SHORE
Bishopville

Bishopville Cemetery is less than a quarter-mile northwest of Bishopville on Maryland 367. The graves are roughly in the center of the cemetery at GPS 38.44884, -75.19683.

In mid-October 1931—in the midst of the harvest—neighbors thought it was odd that none of the Green Davis family was tending the vegetable stand near their Taylorville farmhouse on a busy road. When a fellow farmer investigated, he found Davis, his wife, and their two young daughters shot to death and their modest farmhouse soaked with unlighted kerosene.

Within days, police arrested a black farmhand named Euel Lee, a drifter who had worked for the Davis family but left in a dispute over $1 of wages. At first, Lee (who used the alias Orphan Jones) denied he had killed the family, but after hours of brutal questioning, he confessed that he'd killed them in a drunken rage. Immediately, angry whites on Maryland's rural Eastern Shore were clamoring to lynch Lee, but they were blocked by lawmen.

Lee was tried and convicted by an all-white jury amid Depression-era Jim Crow politics, although appeals dragged on in the racially charged case until October 27, 1933, when Lee was legally hanged. He was buried in the Mount Calvary Cemetery in Brooklyn Park, Maryland, in a section reserved for smallpox victims. His unmarked grave is all but lost somewhere in the area of GPS 39.21250, -76.60374.

For a time, county and state police guarded Lee's grave around the clock to prevent any desecration. But when passions had cooled, the police left and the unmarked grave was forgotten.

The case is examined in detail in former prosecutor Joseph Moore's 2006 book, *Murder on Maryland's Eastern Shore: Race, Politics and the Case of Orphan Jones.*

MYSTERIOUS SERIAL KILLINGS
Cabin John

The Cabin John Bridge is in the Cabin John Creek Regional Park at GPS 38.972795, -77.148668. It is where MacArthur Boulevard crosses the Cabin John Parkway.

On January 18, 1970, a fourteen-year-old girl was found in the undergrowth beneath this bridge, an ice pick in her brain.

Ten days later, a thirty-three-year-old high school teacher was found stabbed more than one hundred times in a car outside her Bethesda apartment (7564 Spring Lake Drive, or GPS 39.027778, -77.153889).

And just five days after that, an eighteen-year-old FBI clerk's body was found slashed and stabbed in her Alexandria high-rise apartment where some two hundred other FBI employees lived.

All the murders happened within a mile of the Beltway in a sixteen-day period. All the victims were young, blond women.

The victim of an unsolved serial killing was found in 1970 beneath the Cabin John Bridge.

Investigators saw further similarities in each attack and presumed they had a serial killer.

But to date, despite FBI involvement, the cases have never been solved and remain open.

A PARENT'S WORST NIGHTMARE
Cape St. Claire

The murder scene is 1242 Mount Pleasant Drive, or GPS 39.037639, -76.448284. This is private property.

On a cold winter morning in 1984, seventeen-year-old Larry Swartz called police to report that his adoptive parents Bob and Kay Swartz had been bludgeoned and stabbed in their home. Devout Catholics and pro-life activists, the Swartzes ran a strict, religious home where they raised three adopted children.

At first, Larry calmly suggested that the murder might have been committed by his adoptive brother Michael, a troubled teenager who'd recently been committed to a mental hospital.

But footprints in the snow and a bloody handprint proved it wasn't Michael who killed the parents. It was Larry.

Larry had been born in New Orleans to a pimp and a teenage hooker, who abandoned him in a suburban Maryland apartment at twenty months old. He spent his next six years in several foster families, where he was abused.

Suffering from a personality disorder and holding long grudges against the Swartzes, Larry had gotten drunk in his room the night before and snapped. Pleading guilty to second-degree murder and sentenced to twelve years in prison, he was released in 1993 and moved to Florida, where he died of a heart attack at age 37 in 2004.

Michael, who'd been cleared of any involvement, was convicted of first-degree murder in an unrelated killing in 1990 and sentenced to life in prison.

The gruesome story is retold in Leslie Walker's 1990 book, *Sudden Fury: A True Story of Adoption and Murder*, and in the 1993 made-for-TV movie, *A Family Torn Apart*, starring Neil Patrick Harris as Larry.

THE CATONSVILLE NINE
Catonsville
The site of the former Catonsville Draft Office (now the Knights of Columbus building) is at 1010 Frederick Road, or GPS 39.270833, -76.738889.

On May 17, 1968, nine anti–Vietnam War protesters—including brothers Daniel and Philip Berrigan, both Catholic priests—entered

Nine Catholic activists, including the Berrigan brothers, burned the Catonsville Draft Board's files here in 1968 to protest the Vietnam War.

the Selective Service Office in the small town of Catonsville, grabbed several boxes full of draft records, and burned them in the parking lot outside with homemade napalm while news cameras rolled.

Although defended by renowned lawyer William Kunstler, all nine were convicted and sentenced from two to six years in prison. But when the time came to go to prison, four of them, including ringleader Father Philip Berrigan (a World War II veteran who had participated in an earlier protest in which he poured blood on Vietnam draft records), went underground. The resulting chase only added more fuel to the counterculture's anti-war flames, and it briefly landed the Berrigans on the FBI's Most Wanted List.

Culling from trial transcripts, Philip's brother Daniel wrote a play, *The Trial of the Catonsville Nine*, which later became a movie.

In 1980, the Berrigans founded the Plowshares Movement, designed to vandalize military and nuclear facilities. All told, Philip spent about eleven years in prison for his various protests.

Philip died from cancer in 2002 at age seventy-nine. He was buried in Baltimore's St. Peter's Cemetery at the Jonah House, 1301 Moreland Avenue; his grave is among a small copse of evergreens at GPS 39.30333, -76.65496. His epitaph: LOVE ONE ANOTHER.

MALE HOOKER CALL CENTER . . . AT SCHOOL
Chevy Chase
Chevy Chase Elementary School is at 4015 Rosemary Street, or GPS 38.97822, -77.080126

You might remember Stephen Gobie as the male prostitute who once worked for openly gay US Rep. Barney Frank (D-Massachusetts), but his rap sheet is far more interesting than his résumé.

By 1989, Gobie had felony convictions for possession of cocaine, oral sodomy, and child porn. Undeterred, he also ran a male prostitution ring out of a borrowed office in the Washington suburbs. Problem is, that borrowed office was . . . an elementary school.

Gobie had a relationship with the school's principal, who allowed the hustler to use a guidance counselor's office at night in 1987 to make appointments with his prostitution clients. The principal resigned under pressure, although the attention-craving Gobie was never prosecuted.

STORY BEHIND *THE EXORCIST*
Cottage City

The actual home of the "haunted boy" whose case inspired the novel and movie *The Exorcist* was 3807 40th Avenue, or GPS 38.938033, -76.951056.

Exorcism might be a common plot device in pop culture, but few actual Catholic exorcisms have ever been done in the US—and it might have caused our national fascination with the ritual, which has boomed in some Protestant faiths.

In 1949, reports of eerie phenomena at a Cottage City house brought a local parish priest to investigate. After a series of strange events in the house, the priest determined that the thirteen-year-old boy who lived there with his family was possessed by a demon, which likely entered him through a Ouija board with which he'd been playing. An exorcism, which typically lasts weeks or months and involves several priests, was approved.

During the nightly ritual, foul messages reportedly appeared on the boy's skin, and he injured one priest while thrashing around. At other times, he cursed, vomited, kicked a priest in the testicles, recited Latin phrases, and caused furniture to shake—or so the scant records of the exorcism allege.

Finally, the boy was declared to be demon-free. A twenty-year-old English major at Georgetown University named William Peter Blatty read the *Washington Post*'s 1949 account ("Priest Frees Mt.

Rainier Boy Reportedly Held in Devil's Grip") and it stuck: In 1971, he fictionalized the story in a novel he called *The Exorcist*, which became a popular film in 1973.

Was the "haunted boy" truly possessed, insane, or just mischievous? We'll likely never know, but several significant sites still exist.

In nearby Mount Rainier, the priest who performed the original rite lived in the rectory of St. James Catholic Church, 3628 Rhode Island Avenue (GPS 38.937905, -76.958236).

After the movie shocked America, rumors flew that a house at 3210 Bunker Hill Road in Mount Rainier (GPS 38.938019, -76.963064) was the scene of the possession. It was a spooky house that later burned to the ground and was never rebuilt—which only added to the mystique. Trouble is, the rumors were wrong. The family that had occupied the house at the time never had children. Today, only a cockeyed set of steps leads to a vacant lot, but the legend persists. If you ask anybody in the area about the "exorcist house," they're likely to point you here, in error.

The real home of the "haunted boy" in Cottage City was only revealed more than fifty years after the exorcism by a dogged local reporter, Mark Opsasnick, who traced the details to find friends and neighbors who confirmed the story about the boy.

The haunting stairway that provided the film's creepiest image is in Washington, right across M Street NW from the Key Bridge, at GPS 38.905473, -77.070202. Originally known as the Hitchcock Steps, this is where the fictional Father Damien Karras (Jason Miller) throws himself from a possessed little girl's bedroom window and tumbles to his death.

A few steps from the top of the stairs is 3600 Prospect Street (GPS 38.905774, -77.070438), the redbrick house where the demonized Regan MacNeil (Linda Blair) lived in the film.

See also "Exorcist Steps" in the Washington, D.C., chapter.

JIMMY'S PLACE
Cottage City

The nightclub sat on the northeast corner of Bladensburg Road and Eastern Avenue NE, or GPS 38.931087, -76.957775.

James LaFontaine, who operated one of the Eastern Seaboard's plushest gambling joints here from the 1920s to the 1940s, understood the secret to a successful criminal operation: location, location, location. His underground club, known as Jimmy's Place, was situated just a few feet beyond the District of Columbia boundary in a Victorian mansion surrounded by a tall green fence. Legend has it that when Maryland cops came knocking, his patrons could quickly scoot across the line into the District, and vice versa. Making a case against LaFontaine was so hard, they say, that both jurisdictions eventually gave up entirely until the place was closed for good in 1947. LaFontaine died in 1949.

HOMICIDE OR HONOR?
Cumberland

Rose Hill Cemetery is at 535 Fayette Street, or GPS 39.653207, -78.774955.

Colonel William McKaig (1842–1870) was a wealthy industrialist and a former Confederate officer. Henry Black worked for a coal mine and was a former Confederate, too. But they nursed hatred for each other in the small town of Cumberland.

Their mutual antagonism arose from an intimate fact: The married cad McKaig had secretly impregnated Black's sister during a long affair and had later bad-mouthed her as a prostitute to unsuspecting neighbors.

So on October 17, 1870, Black hunted down McKaig near the intersection of Mechanic and Baltimore Streets (GPS 39.651123, -78.763526) and shot him three times in front of astounded citizens, shouting, "Now, seduce another sister of mine!"

McKaig died on the spot and was buried in a family plot at Rose Hill Cemetery's Section 4, Lot 12, or GPS 39.65497, -78.77540.

On trial for murder, Black claimed he was merely defending his sister's honor against a lusty scoundrel. The jury was out only one hour: not guilty.

Black lived many more years in Cumberland, dying in 1921 at age seventy-eight. He was also buried at Rose Hill, in Section 8, Lot 1A, or GPS 39.65527, -78.77622.

A SCHOOLGIRL'S MURDER
Denton

Denton Cemetery is on Meeting House Road, a half-mile west of Denton across the Choptank River. The killer's grave is on the western side of the cemetery, just off Maryland 328, at GPS 38.88923, -75.84285.

On March 26, 1895, thirteen-year-old Sallie Dean was walking down a dirt road to school near the village of Harmony, south of Denton. Along the way, she met a killer. Later that day, Sallie's father found her corpse hidden among some trees. Her throat had been slashed, and she'd been raped.

Local cops were clueless, so they asked some Baltimore detectives for help. They quickly identified a suspect: Marshall Price, a twenty-three-year-old married blacksmith who lived along the road and had actually helped search for Sallie. In fact, Price was the searcher who found the murder weapon, a long knife, hidden in the small grove.

At first, Price claimed he was innocent, but when he was safely in jail, he confessed to the murder. Why? He worried that he might be lynched if he'd admitted his deed before he was locked up.

Alas, he was wrong. On July 2, some forty masked men broke into the Caroline County Jail (much renovated but still standing at 101 Gay Street in Denton, or GPS 38.887633, -75.833712) and hanged Price from a nearby maple tree. When Price's corpse was cut down, the fatal rope was chopped into souvenir pieces and handed out to onlookers.

Price's grave in Denton Cemetery is oriented differently (east-west) than all the other graves in the Denton Cemetery (north-south). Price's body was laid so that "when he rises on Judgment Day, his back will be to his Maker."

Sallie Dean was buried in Federalsburg's Hillcrest Cemetery at 101 Bloomingdale Avenue behind First Church of God. Her epitaph simply says, MURDERED. The grave is in Section D-50 at GPS 38.70056, -75.77718.

Child-killer Marshall Price was deliberately buried perpendicular to the proper folks of Denton, Maryland.

SUBURBAN SPREE KILLER
Dundalk

The crime scene is at 7520 Lange Street, or GPS 39.286746, -76.508253.

Joseph Palczynski (1968–2000) was a bad dude with a bad attitude. An unemployed electrician and bodybuilder, he'd done time for several domestic assaults and was on parole when he was arrested again in 2000 for beating his girlfriend in the rural Baltimore suburb of Bowley's Quarters. His arrest triggered violent revenge.

After bonding out of jail, Palczynski went directly to a home where his estranged girlfriend had taken refuge. There, he grabbed his girlfriend, killing the couple that protected her and a bystander. Then he killed a young mother during a failed carjacking.

After ten days on the run, taking other hostages briefly along the way, Palczynski's girlfriend-hostage escaped. He then broke into the Dundalk home of his girlfriend's mother, where he held three people hostage for an astonishing ninety-seven hours as local TV cameras rolled nonstop.

The hostages escaped after spiking Palczynski's iced tea with a knock-out drug. Police quickly stormed the house and shot Palczynski twenty-seven times. He died.

MURDER IN THE CIA?
Frederick

Mount Olivet Cemetery is at 515 South Market Street. Frank Rudolph Olson's grave is in Section RR, Lot 37, or GPS 39.40039, -77.41979.

Frank Olson (1910–1953) was a CIA bio-weapons specialist working at Fort Detrick, Maryland, on top-secret mind-control and biological weapons. On November 19, 1953, during a meeting of CIA and Fort Detrick scientists at Deep Creek Lodge in rural Maryland,

Olson's cocktail was spiked with LSD. He emerged from his "trip" angry and agitated enough to resign from his job.

But his bosses wouldn't accept his resignation. Instead, they took him to New York, ostensibly for psychiatric help. Even more frustrated after being examined by a CIA allergist and a magician, he wandered Manhattan and threw away his wallet containing all his identification before eating Thanksgiving dinner in an automat. The next day, the CIA decided Olson should be committed to a mental hospital.

That night, forty-three-year-old Olson plunged ten stories from Room 1018A at New York's Statler Hotel and died on the sidewalk below. The CIA said Olson, depressed and disturbed by his LSD dosing, had fallen or jumped from the window.

But when a CIA report in the 1970s suggested there might have been more to the story, Olson's family was shocked. Some of them believed Olson might have been murdered to cover up secret programs about which the angry scientist knew too much. Nevertheless,

Was CIA agent Frank Olson's death a suicide . . . or a murder?

the family accepted a $750,000 settlement in 1976 and agreed never to sue the government.

A 1994 autopsy on Olson's exhumed body showed head and chest injuries that were not caused by the fall; forensic scientist James Starrs called the new evidence "rankly and starkly suggestive of homicide." In 1996, the Manhattan district attorney opened a murder investigation into Olson's death, but no charges were ever filed.

The case has been explored extensively in TV shows such as *Unsolved Mysteries* and *Dr. G's Most Shocking Cases*.

ANTHRAX TERROR
Frederick

The late Dr. Bruce Ivins's home is at 622 Military Road, or GPS 39.432548, -77.427251. This is private property.

In late 2001, while America was still reeling from the September 11 terror attacks, a new threat shook a frightened public. Envelopes containing powdered anthrax had been mailed to news organizations and two US senators, infecting twenty-two people and killing five as the nation's largest bioterror attack crippled the Postal Service, closed a Senate office building for three months, and shut down the House of Representatives for a week.

At first, the FBI focused on an Army scientist who had been under constant surveillance for several years. Agents consulted Dr. Bruce Ivins of the US Army's Medical Research Institute of Infectious Diseases at Maryland's Fort Detrick (GPS 39.435278, -77.428333) and one of the nation's best anthrax researchers. Ivins had even occasionally offered theories accusing some of his own colleagues of the anthrax mailings.

But when new science found traceable genetic codes in anthrax spores that led to Ivins's lab, the FBI suddenly had a new target: Ivins himself. The *Los Angeles Times* surmised that Ivins stood to profit from the anthrax scare because he held two patents on an anthrax vaccine, but others believed he was motivated by revenge against real and imagined enemies.

In July 2008, just as the FBI was about to accuse Ivins of the attack, he committed suicide at his home with an overdose of sleep medicine. He was sixty-two, and his body was cremated.

A portrait of the deeply troubled scientist with a secret life emerged. After a traumatic childhood, Ivins had developed an obsession with a college sorority after being rebuffed by a member for a date in college. He had burglarized sorority offices, stalked people, and made long night trips to mail packages—all while hiding his mental issues from bosses who could revoke his security clearances. Just before he was to be charged in the anthrax case, the FBI believes Ivins planned a mass murder so he could "go out in a blaze of glory."

Many of Ivins's colleagues remain convinced he played no role in the anthrax attacks. They have raised doubts as to whether he had either the intention or the ability to weaponize anthrax, but the FBI still believes Ivins was the killer.

A RIDE ON THE LEGAL CAROUSEL
Glen Echo

The Glen Echo amusement park is at 7300 MacArthur Boulevard, or GPS 38.966995, -77.138239.

Before 1961, only white folks could grab for the brass ring on the historic Dentzel carousel in Glen Echo Park, an amusement park that first opened in 1898.

But that all began to change on a summer day in 1960, when five Howard University students protested the park's segregationist policies by riding the carousel and were arrested for trespassing by a sheriff's deputy who was moonlighting as a park security guard.

The students—four men and a woman—were convicted and fined $100 each. But as antisegregation protests grew more intense at Glen Echo Park's front gate (and across America), the park's owners decided in 1961 to admit all races.

Meanwhile, the students' case made its way to the US Supreme Court in 1964, where justices ruled 6-3 that the arrest by a moonlighting deputy was effectively a "state action" that violated the Equal Protection Clause of the 14th Amendment. The case, known as *Griffin v. Maryland,* was one of the last such cases decided before Congress passed the 1964 Civil Rights Act to outlaw segregation in all forms.

Glen Echo Park closed its gates in 1968 but reopened in 1971 as an arts and cultural park under the auspices of the National Park Service.

The carousel is still there, but it's the last functioning ride in the park (GPS 38.966198, -77.138856). Built by the Dentzel Carousel Company in 1921, it is one of 135 still-functioning antique

The historic carousel in Glen Echo Park was the scene of a landmark protest against segregation laws.

carousels in the country. It is nothing if not a whimsical symbol of inclusion with its thirty-eight multicolored horses, four rabbits, four ostriches, a lion, a tiger, a giraffe, and deer. Alas, the carousel's original brass ring game, in which riders had a chance to grab a small ring of brass to get a free ride, is no longer played, but its hardware remains.

BELTWAY SNIPER
Glenmont

While the Beltway Sniper shootings happened in many places in Maryland, Washington, and Virginia, the bloodiest thirty hours began in the parking lot of the Shoppers Food Warehouse, 2210 Randolph Road, or GPS 39.059881, -77.047366.

During three weeks in October 2002, a deadly sniper terrorized Washington suburbs in Maryland and Virginia, killing ten innocent people and wounding three others in a bloody binge of long-distance shootings that paralyzed the Beltway.

Menacingly enough, it began with a bullet that missed. On October 2, while a Glenmont hobby-shop clerk rang up a purchase around 5:20 p.m., a bullet smashed through a window and ricocheted off a cash-register sign.

But less than an hour later, fifty-five-year-old James Martin was killed by a single shot to his chest when he got out of his car at the Shoppers Food Warehouse near one of the county's busiest intersections.

Martin's death was a tragedy, but it was the murder of five random people the next day that convinced police they had a serial shooter.

At 7:41 a.m. on October 3, Sonny Buchanan, a thirty-nine-year-old landscaper, was shot in the back while he mowed a small patch of lawn at the Fitzgerald Auto Mall, 11411 Rockville Pike, or GPS 39.043056, -77.110556.

A half-hour later, part-time taxi driver Premkumar Walekar was killed while he pumped gas at a nearby Mobil station, 4100 Aspen Hill Road, in Silver Spring (GPS 39.079822, -77.081132).

Then within minutes, housekeeper Sarah Ramos was shot to death as she sat reading a book on a bus-stop bench at the Leisure World Shopping Center, 3802 International Boulevard in Silver Spring (GPS 39.102206, -77.075272).

The morning's slaughter ended just before 10 a.m. when twenty-five-year-old Lori Ann Lewis-Rivera was killed while vacuuming her minivan at a Shell station, 10515 Connecticut Avenue in Kensington (GPS 39.02799, -77.076121).

But the gruesome day wasn't over. A little after 9 p.m., a retired carpenter named Pascal Charlot was mortally wounded as he crossed Georgia Avenue at Kalmia Road, in Washington, D.C. (GPS 38.983927, -77.026439).

Over the next few weeks, four more people died and three were wounded by the unseen shooter, now being dubbed the Beltway Sniper, who'd also left taunting notes for police at one scene. The victims were white, black, Indian, male, female, young, and old. Among them:

On October 9, Dean Harold Meyers, fifty-four, was killed while filling his car at Pump #4 at a Sunoco gas station, 7203 Sudley Road near Manassas, Virginia (GPS 38.797672, -77.517664).

On October 11, Kenneth Bridges, fifty-three, was killed while pumping gas at the Exxon station at Exit 126 on Interstate 95 near Fredericksburg, Virginia (GPS 38.244143, -77.498412).

On October 14, at 9:15 p.m., FBI analyst Linda Franklin, forty-seven, was killed in the Home Depot parking garage at the Seven Corners Shopping Center in Falls Church, Virginia (GPS 38.8692, -77.149585).

On October 22, bus driver Conrad Johnson, forty, was killed as he stood on the steps of his bus at a stop in the 14100 block of Grande Pre Road in Silver Spring (GPS 39.092726, -77.07626).

It all came to an end on October 24 when an ex-soldier named John Allen Muhammad and his teenage accomplice Boyd Lee Malvo were arrested at an Interstate 70 rest stop (on the north side of the highway at Exit 39, or GPS 39.524444, -77.600556), asleep in a blue 1990 Caprice modified to let them fire their rifle through a loophole in the trunk.

Prosecutors believe the angry racist Muhammad had planned to extort millions of dollars in blood money to start a new nation of black separatists in Canada, or maybe even to ultimately kill his estranged wife so he could have custody of his children.

After trials in Maryland and Virginia, Muhammad was sentenced to die, and Malvo got life in prison. Muhammad waived his appeals and was executed by lethal injection in Jarratt, Virginia, on November 10, 2009. He was forty-eight, and his cremated ashes were given to his son in Louisiana.

Sniper John Allen Muhammad

A memorial to the Beltway Sniper's victims was erected at Brookside Botanical Gardens, 1800 Glenallan Avenue in Wheaton, Maryland (GPS 39.057148, -77.036919).

This memorial at Brookside Botanical Gardens in Wheaton pays tribute to the victims of the Beltway Snipers.

HELL HOUSE
Ilchester

The ruins of old St. Mary's College are scattered over several acres in a dense woodland in Patapsco Valley State Park, just west of where the Ilchester Road crosses the Patapsco River. The overgrown campus area is centered around GPS 39.250556, -76.765833. This is private property.

Not all legends are urban. Some—like those swirling around "Hell House" —are decidedly rural. Most are variations of a yarn about an insane priest who hanged five young girls facing one another around a pentagram and then shot himself. It never happened, but the legend of such a ghastly crime (and of satanic rituals, meth labs, and malicious caretakers) fuels the old seminary's nickname: Hell House.

St. Mary's College began as a seminary built by a Roman Catholic religious order called the Redemptorists in 1866. It operated until 1972, when it closed because nobody attended the school anymore. The large, spooky brick structures fell into ruins, and a series of fires made the cavernous old hulks dangerous. A gun-toting caretaker with vicious dogs guarded it for many years, but he might have only added an extra thrill to vandals and trespassing kids who embellished the old ghost stories.

The State of Maryland bulldozed most of the abandoned buildings in 2006 for safety reasons.

Not much remains of "Hell House," as the ruins of St. Mary's College in Ilchester are known today. AMY McGOVERN

GEORGE WALLACE GUNNED DOWN
Laurel

The would-be assassination site now sits under a bank building in the parking lot of the Laurel Shopping Center, or GPS 39.096232, -76.854574.

Alabama Governor George C. Wallace (1919–1998) was a candidate for the Democratic presidential nomination when he delivered a campaign speech in the parking lot of the Laurel Shopping Center on May 15, 1972. An ardent opponent of desegregation (but a one-time favorite of the NAACP), Wallace led Alabama through its dark days of the civil-rights struggle but emerged a popular but polarizing force in American politics of the early 1970s.

As Wallace finished his Laurel speech, he stepped from behind his bulletproof shield to mingle with supporters. A blond young man hollered several times, "Hey, George, over here!" As Wallace came closer, the blond man—a twenty-one-year-old unemployed janitor named Arthur Bremer—shoved his .38 revolver into Wallace's belly and emptied the cylinder, hitting Wallace four times and wounding three bystanders.

Wallace was rushed into emergency surgery at Holy Cross Hospital in Silver Spring (1500 Forest Glen Road, or GPS 39.015, -77.035278), but doctors were unable to remove a bullet lodged near his spine. He was paralyzed below the chest for the rest of his life.

Bremer, who had stalked Wallace for weeks, was convicted of attempted murder and sentenced to sixty-three years in prison. After only thirty-five years, he was paroled in 2007 and is last known to have been living in Maryland.

Although wheelchair-bound, Wallace was twice more elected governor of Alabama and ran for president in 1976, although his opponents hit hard on his disability. In a 1995 letter, Wallace forgave Bremer. He died in 1998 at age seventy-nine and is buried in Montgomery, Alabama.

In the 1976 film *Taxi Driver,* director Martin Scorsese loosely based the character of would-be Travis Bickle on Bremer—which, in turn, inspired would-be Reagan assassin John Hinckley.

See also "President Ronald Reagan Shot" (Washington, D.C.).

AN ALL-WOMAN JURY . . . IN 1656
Lusby

A historical marker exists near the site of the murder trial, the former General Provincial Court at Patuxent, at the intersection of Maryland Routes 765 and 2/4 (GPS 38.41585, -76.457017).

Indentured servant Judith Catchpole was barely off the ship *Mary and Francis* when she was accused by a fellow passenger of witchcraft and of killing her own baby on the long journey. The man claimed Catchpole had given birth aboard the ship, then murdered her child. Just for good measure, he claimed she had also slit a woman's throat and stabbed a sailor . . . then used her magical powers to heal their wounds. Catchpole passionately denied the tale and said she'd never been pregnant.

An all-female jury—seven single and four married women—was empaneled. Why? Common law and colonial justice took a pragmatic view that a jury should be able to expertly judge the facts. In this case, the judge decided women were better able to determine whether Judith Catchpole was telling the truth.

As the law had intended, after a private examination, these women quickly saw that Catchpole had never been pregnant. They acquitted her of all charges.

This was not the first all-woman jury on American soil, but it was extremely rare for the next 264 years, until the Nineteenth Amendment was ratified in 1920.

THE HARDEST HEART
Middle River

The crime scene is a former convenience store in the 9000 block of Pulaski Highway, or GPS 39.345281, -76.465434.

John Thanos (1951–1994) was a sadistic armed robber and spree killer convicted of robbing and murdering a teenage clerk and his girlfriend during a Labor Day 1990 holdup at the Big Red gasoline station in Middle River, and of the cold-blooded slaying of a teenager who had given Thanos a ride. He was arrested after a lengthy gun battle.

As monstrous as his crimes had been, Thanos saved his most monstrous behavior for his trial, where he jeered his victims' families and wished aloud that he could defile their corpses all over again:

"Their cries bring laughter from the darkest caverns of my soul," he said at his sentencing. "I don't believe I could satisfy my thirst yet in this matter unless I was to be able to dig these brats' bones up out of their graves right now and beat them into powder and urinate on them and then stir it into a murky yellowish elixir and serve it up to those loved ones."

Waiving all death-penalty appeals, Thanos was executed by lethal injection two years after his conviction, the one-thousandth killer to be executed in the US since 1976. His last word: "Adios."

THRILL-KILLING BY THE SEA
Ocean City

The Rainbow Condominiums are at 11200 Coastal Highway, or GPS 38.41843, -75.056107.

Erika and Benjamin Sifrit saw themselves as a cool, modern-day Bonnie and Clyde. She was a former honor student and college basketball player who liked living on the edge; he was a former Navy SEAL with a taste for tattoos and blood.

The two twentysomethings supported their lavish, clubbing lifestyle by burglarizing homes and selling their booty on eBay. On Memorial Day weekend 2002, the Pennsylvania couple was planning a two-week burglary spree in Ocean City.

On a transit bus to an oceanfront club called Seacrets (117 49th Street, or GPS 38.374533, -75.071812), the Sifrits met Joshua Ford and his girlfriend, Martha Crutchley. The four ended up later at the Sifrits' rented penthouse at the Rainbow Condominiums for hot-tubbing and drinks.

In a bizarre turn of events, the Sifrits attacked the unsuspecting couple, who locked themselves in the bathroom. But the Sifrits battered down the door and killed Ford and Crutchley. They were stripped of their valuables and their bodies were dismembered, stuffed in plastic garbage bags, and tossed in a grocery store dumpster in Rehoboth Beach, twenty-seven miles away. Pieces of Ford and Crutchley were found later in a Delaware landfill.

When the Sifrits were arrested a week later while burglarizing a Hooters restaurant (12207 Coastal Highway, or GPS 38.427796, -75.056062), the macabre murder unraveled—and each blamed the other for the killings. Benjamin said Erika did all the killing and he merely chopped up the bodies; Erika claimed Benjamin—who'd plotted to kill his wife's entire family for the inheritance—terrorized and killed the frightened couple, then got a tattoo to remind himself of the bloody night.

Two juries didn't buy it. Benjamin got thirty-five years in prison for second-degree murder and other crimes related to the slayings; Erika got life-plus-twenty years for first-degree murder.

In 2008, Benjamin filed for divorce from Erika. Grounds? Because Erika, he said, was a convicted felon. It was granted.

HENRY LEE LUCAS IN MARYLAND
Port Deposit

The former Best Western/World Inns Motel (now a Ramada Limited) is at 6422 Baltimore National Pike in Catonsville, or GPS 39.284864, -76.758165.

One of America's most twisted serial killers lived for a time in a small Maryland town and confessed to killing at least one Marylander, although he never spent a day in prison for the murder.

One-eyed itinerant psychopath Henry Lee Lucas (1936–2001) killed at least five people—including his mother—and confessed controversially to hundreds. He partnered with transvestite-cannibal Ottis Toole (who killed Adam Walsh, son of victim advocate and TV host John Walsh) in 1976, but they split up after Lucas started living with Toole's seven-year-old niece . . . who later turned up dismembered.

But in 1975, Lucas was living in Port Deposit. On December 5, 1975, while renting a small house at 1 Granite Avenue (GPS 39.613782, -76.125732), he married girlfriend Betty M. Crawford.

A week later, a forty-nine-year-old Lochearn restaurateur named James Carpellotti was found strangled in Room 253 at the Best Western Motel. His wallet containing $40 and some jewelry were missing, and police had no idea who might have killed the co-owner of the popular Danti's restaurant on Liberty Road (now defunct).

A couple months later, Lucas and his bride rented a trailer at Benjamin's Trailer Park (now the far western portion of Homestead Mobile Home Park, 4 Homestead Drive, at GPS 39.621092, -76.097403). He made money by occasionally borrowing cash from the owner and by helping his junk-dealer brother-in-law Wade Kiser sell scrap metal from his junkyard on rural Linton Run Road (GPS 39.621365, -76.050485).

Through 1976–77, Lucas was frequently on the road, and bodies were piling up in places as far away as Texas. Sometime around the end of 1977, he left Maryland for good. In 1983, he was arrested by

Texas Rangers for unlawful gun possession—and Lucas was soon linked to several murders.

Lucas pleaded guilty and began spilling confessions to hundreds of other murders. Among them was the killing of James Carpellotti. Although many of Lucas's confessions were later debunked, Baltimore homicide detectives found he knew things about Carpellotti's killing that only the murderer would know. The drifter claimed he had gone to the motel with Carpellotti for sex, then killed him when the married father of one refused to pay for it. Lucas was indicted in 1984 but never extradited from Texas to stand trial in Maryland.

In all, Lucas was convicted in eleven murders and sent to Death Row for killing an unidentified Texas woman known only as "Orange Socks" because of socks found with her remains. But his death sentence, clouded by many questions, was commuted by Gov. George W. Bush in 1998, and Lucas died in prison of heart failure in 2001 at age sixty-four. His unclaimed body was buried in the Huntsville (Texas) prison cemetery, Peckerwood Hill (GPS 320.71222, -95.53595).

MARYLAND'S LAST LYNCHING
Princess Anne
The courthouse lawn where the lynching happened is at 30512 Prince William Street, or GPS 38.204337, -75.693709.

On October 16, 1933, an elderly white woman on an evening walk was attacked by a black man on a farm road. Witnesses heard her screams and rushed to the spot, where the woman immediately identified her attacker as twenty-three-year-old laborer George Armwood.

Armwood was arrested, but fearing a lynch mob might form, he was held in Baltimore until the early morning hours of October 17, when he was secretly brought to Princess Anne's jail.

Over the next three days, an angry mob of more than one thousand people gathered around the jail, battering its doors with heavy timbers. They ultimately snatched Armwood, who was hiding beneath his mattress, and dragged him out to be beaten, stabbed, and kicked on the way to a nearby tree, where he was hoisted with a rope. When he was dead, his corpse was taken back to the courthouse lawn, strung from a telephone pole, and burned before being dumped in a local lumberyard.

Princess Anne wanted to believe the lynching was done by outsiders, but it was, in fact, organized locally. Two years later, twelve lynchers were identified, but when they came to their first hearing, hundreds of supporters cheered as the judge dismissed all charges.

PATTY CANNON'S FARM
Reliance

A historical marker exists on the site of Patty Cannon's farm, on the northwest corner of the intersection of Maryland Routes 392 and 577 (GPS 38.635431, -75.708182).

Part mobster, part kidnapper, and pure wickedness, Patty Cannon (1760–1829) was one of America's most dreadful female killers.

She was the matriarch of a gang that kidnapped free blacks and sold them into slavery. She ran a brutal but profitable operation that eluded justice by merely jumping back and forth over the Maryland-Delaware state line, a stone's throw from her home and tavern.

In 1829, a farmer plowing the fields on Cannon's land unearthed the clandestine grave of a rival slave trader that Cannon had always been rumored to have killed. Authorities quickly found more graves, including two children and a baby.

Delaware charged Cannon with four counts of murder, but before her trial, Cannon committed suicide in prison. She was buried in a pauper's grave beside the jail.

In 1907, her remains were exhumed for a jail expansion and her skull secretly stolen. Years later, it was delivered to the Dover (Delaware) Public Library, where it remains today.

Rumors have swirled for years that the Patty Cannon gang had buried up to $100,000 in gold coins in furtive caches throughout the area. In fact, treasure hunters in the 1950s found some hoards of gold coins, some in glass jars, just a few feet from where Cannon's tavern once stood.

The historical marker here isn't exactly accurate. The house you see wasn't hers. Historians have shown that Cannon's actual home was several hundred yards away, although she owned this parcel of land. Her real house, built sometime in the 1700s, was torn down in 1948.

Patty Cannon and her murderous eighteenth-century gang wreaked havoc in the Maryland countryside.

AMERICAN LITERATURE'S GREATEST MURDER
Rockville

St. Mary's Cemetery is at the intersection of Veirs Mill and Old Baltimore Roads. The Fitzgeralds' graves are at GPS 39.08196, -77.14537.

If you haven't yet read the classic 1925 novel *The Great Gatsby*, be forewarned: This little snippet might spoil it for you . . . or it might intrigue you enough to pick it up.

Arguably, the murder of Jay Gatsby in Fitzgerald's Jazz Age masterwork is American literature's most profound and consequential homicide (and if you're a student, feel free to explore that theme in English class). Gatsby's ironic, undignified killing stands in contrast to everything he symbolized about the American dream.

And Gatsby's killer—at least in the literary sense—was author F. Scott Fitzgerald, one of the great literary lights of the twentieth century.

F. Scott Fitzgerald

The author of *Tender Is the Night* and *This Side of Paradise* had some family ties to Maryland and lived with his wife, Zelda, for a time at 1307 Park Avenue in Baltimore (GPS 39.306396, -76.623298), among other local places.

When he died of a heart attack in 1940 at age forty-four in Los Angeles, the Catholic Church denied his wish to be buried beside his parents in St. Mary's Cemetery because he was not a practicing Catholic and because his books had been officially condemned by the church. So he was buried in Rockville's Union Cemetery.

But in 1975, his only daughter, Scottie, won approval to exhume him and Zelda (who had died in a 1948 fire in the North Carolina mental hospital where she was institutionalized with schizophrenia) and rebury them in the Fitzgerald family plot at St. Mary's.

F. Scott Fitzgerald just might have authored American literature's most important murder.

Fittingly, the capstone over the Fitzgerald gravesite bears the closing line from *The Great Gatsby*: SO WE BEAT ON, BOATS AGAINST THE CURRENT, BORNE BACK CEASELESSLY INTO THE PAST.

Fitzgerald's life is examined in Matthew Bruccoli's 2002 biography, *Some Sort of Epic Grandeur: The Life of F. Scott Fitzgerald*.

CROSS-DRESSING CANNIBAL KILLER UNMASKED
Silver Spring

Victim Michelle Dorr's home is at 9129 Sudbury Road, or GPS 39.007057, -77.006329.

Hadden Clark (b. 1952) was born to abusive, alcoholic parents in Connecticut. His drunken mother would often dress him in little girls' dresses, and his father would beat him mercilessly for being a "retard" and showing effeminate tendencies. But Clark embraced all his proclivities: He grew to like wearing women's clothes, torturing pets, and bullying other kids. Although he trained as a chef at the Culinary Institute of America, he drifted from job to job and was eventually booted from the Navy after being diagnosed as a paranoid schizophrenic who wore fancy women's underwear under his uniform.

Clark then went to live with his older brother, Geoffrey, in Silver Spring, but it didn't last long. On May 31, 1986, Clark was kicked out of the house for masturbating in front of his young niece.

That same day, six-year-old Michele Dorr was last seen alive walking out the back door of her house on Sudbury Road to swim in a plastic pool outside—just two doors down from Geoffrey Clark's house, where her best friend lived. When she went to her friend's house, Clark lured her into his room and stabbed her with one of his chef's knives before bundling her in a duffel bag and burying her in a shallow grave at a local park. He later admitted to eating some of her flesh and trying unsuccessfully to have sex with the corpse. He was questioned by police but had an alibi.

Clark didn't hit police radar again until 1992, when he was living in his truck in the parking lot of Bethesda's United Methodist Church (8300 Old Georgetown Road, or GPS 38.993529, -77.108563) and working as a private gardener for a Bethesda psychiatrist. Around midnight on October 17, he sneaked into the family home at Julliard Drive and Ashburton Lane (GPS 39.019485, -77.124879) and went into the bedroom of the psychiatrist's daughter, Laura Houghteling. Dressed in women's clothing, he woke the girl and forced her at gunpoint to undress and take a bath. He then smothered her by covering her mouth with duct tape and buried her in a secret grave.

When Clark's fingerprints matched a bloody handprint on a pillowcase he'd kept as a souvenir, he was arrested. He pleaded guilty to second-degree murder and got thirty years in prison—where he unwisely bragged about Michele Dorr's killing years earlier. After Clark led cops to Dorr's and Houghteling's graves, DNA subsequently linked him to the little girl's killing, too, and he got an extra sixty years.

Killer Hadden Clark

Since being at the Western Correctional Institution in Cumberland (GPS 39.606667, -78.815278), Clark has told investigators he killed up to twelve women and girls along the Eastern Seaboard from the mid-'70s to his capture in 1993. In 2000, Clark told police about a special hoard of "trophies" he'd collected from his victims. On land his grandfather once owned, cops subsequently found a bucket containing about two hundred pieces of women's jewelry, including Laura Houghteling's class ring.

Hadden Clark's story is examined in detail in Adrian Havil's 2001 book, *Born Evil: A True Story of Cannibalism and Serial Murder.*

DISCOVERY CHANNEL GRUDGE
Silver Spring

DCI World headquarters is at 1 Discovery Place, or GPS 38.995664, -77.02799.

James J. Lee (1967–2010) harbored a grudge. He believed the Discovery Channel was hastening the end of the earth, not delaying it. He had mounted several protests at the channel's Silver Spring headquarters, and he wrote a ranting manifesto that said, in part: "Nothing is more important than saving . . . the Lions, Tigers, Giraffes, Elephants, Froggies, Turtles, Apes, Raccoons, Beetles, Ants, Sharks, Bears, and, of course, the Squirrels. The humans? The planet does not need humans."

On the sunny afternoon of September 1, 2010, the mentally ill native Hawaiian Lee strolled into the building with a gun and several parcels, later found to be homemade bombs. Ordering everyone to freeze, he said he had bombs before taking three hostages in the first-floor lobby. Later, he told two of his hostages, "Today is a good day to die."

After four hours of negotiating, Silver Spring SWAT snipers killed Lee when he fired at hostages trying to escape.

LOCATION, LOCATION, LOCATION
Silver Spring
The house is at 9337 Columbia Boulevard, or GPS 39.008653, -77.03938. This is private property.

In 2002, a wig-wearing intruder crawled through the window of this two-story redbrick colonial and shot to death a nine-year-old girl and her father. The killer was convicted and sentenced to life in prison.

The house, however, had unsettled issues. Brian Betts, a forty-five-year-old teacher, bought the house in 2003, never knowing what had happened there. But when he found out from neighbors, he immediately contacted his real-estate agent, who hadn't known the house's history either. To appease Betts, an exorcism was performed by two priests, and Betts's anxiety was relieved.

Unfortunately, Betts was also murdered in the house in 2010. Four teenagers were arrested and pleaded guilty to the robbery-slaying.

FAMILY-KILLING FOR HIRE
Silver Spring
The murder scene is a home at 13502 Northgate Drive, or GPS 39.084685, -77.046811. This is private property.

Lawrence Horn had been a pioneer producer during Motown Records' heyday in the late 1960s, but after being laid off in the 1990s, he was swamped in debt. He had divorced his wife, Mildred, and was suing to inherit a $1.7 million medical-malpractice settlement held by his severely mentally disabled eight-year-old son, Trevor, who'd been rendered a quadriplegic by a hospital accident during his birth.

Then on March 3, 1993, Mildred was murdered in her Silver Spring home with a single shot to the eye by a .22-caliber rifle.

Next, Trevor's overnight nurse was killed the same way. And finally, Trevor was smothered in his bed.

But Lawrence Horn had an alibi. At the very moment of the killings, he was in Los Angeles, conveniently playing with a video camera that recorded the exact time and date.

However, police linked Horn to a hired killer named James Perry, who had been staying in Silver Spring the night of the killings. As the complex web unraveled, police found that Perry was hired by Horn and had recently purchased a book titled *Hit Man* and followed it precisely in the slaying spree.

Perry was convicted and given three death sentences but died of an undisclosed illness in prison in 2009; Horn got three life sentences. After a lawsuit was filed, the publisher of *Hit Man* paid millions in a settlement to the victims' families and stopped selling the book.

A WHODUNIT PLAY AND A REAL MURDER
St. Michaels

The Harbourtowne Resort is at 9784 Mattingham Circle. Cottage #506 is at GPS 38.82092, -76.23062.

It should have been a romantic Valentine's Day getaway: Stephen and Kimberly Hricko of Laurel wanted to prop up their sagging marriage by attending a murder-mystery weekend at a swanky resort on Maryland's Eastern Shore in 1998. They would see *The Bride Who Cried*, an interactive play in which a newlywed poisons her groom at their wedding, and the audience is invited to help solve the case.

But the murder Kimberly had in mind wasn't fictional. She had a young lover and wanted out of her marriage, but she could get a $400,000 life insurance payout if her husband died accidentally. Her plan was worthy of a Broadway play: She had stolen a vial of succinylcholine—a powerful muscle relaxant that can halt a person's breathing in seconds and is practically undetectable—from the hospital where she worked as a surgical technician. She also bought a pack of cheap cigars.

After the play, the Hrickos returned to Cottage 506 where Kimberly injected her husband with the drug, then set fire to the room's drapes. By the time firefighters arrived, the room was engulfed. They found Stephen's badly burned body on the bed.

It might have been the perfect crime except that friends told police after Stephen's death that Kimberly had told them she wanted to kill her husband. She had even tried to hire a co-worker to do it.

Kimberly was eventually convicted of first-degree murder and arson and sentenced to life in prison. Stephen was buried in State College, Pennsylvania.

Today, resort guests often ask specifically for the room where Stephen Hricko died.

THE FALL OF SPIRO AGNEW
Timonium

Dulaney Valley Memorial Gardens is at 200 East Padonia Road. The grave is in Section 2, Garden of the Last Supper, at GPS 39.45744, -76.61983.

Spiro T. Agnew (1918–1996) had an impressive résumé. The son of a Greek immigrant educated in Baltimore public schools, he served during both World War II and Korea, earned a law degree from the University of Baltimore Law School, and won several local government seats before being elected Maryland's governor in 1966. Two years later, he was tapped as Richard Nixon's running mate in the 1968 elections and won the vice presidency. Four years later, he won reelection, too.

But then Agnew's charmed life began to crumble. Charged with accepting bribes while he was the governor of Maryland and falsifying federal tax returns, Agnew pleaded no contest and resigned October 10, 1973. In 1983, he repaid $268,482 to the State of Maryland—the amount of bribes he allegedly accepted while in the governor's mansion (100 State Circle in Annapolis, at GPS 38.978907, -76.491889).

Agnew died of leukemia in Ocean City, Maryland, in 1996 at age seventy-seven. He was cremated and his ashes buried at Dulaney Valley Memorial Gardens in Timonium. His headstone makes no reference to his political career.

4

ARLINGTON NATIONAL CEMETERY

It is America's most hallowed ground. At rest here amid the gently rolling hills of northern Virginia are three hundred thousand American veterans and their families, including two presidents, beloved politicians, famous war heroes, sports stars, scientists, explorers, judges, doctors, authors, astronauts, entertainers, and—maybe surprisingly—more than a few people who played significant roles in American crime history.

Although now a sacred place, Arlington was once a grim potter's field, not the 624-acre Elysian field you see today.

At its zenith, the bloody Civil War was grinding out more dead than the local cemeteries could hold. So in 1864, the US quartermaster general—a Southerner who remained loyal to the Union—proposed to turn Confederate General Robert E. Lee's abandoned Arlington estate into a graveyard. The *Washington Post* once described the unkempt, bleak pastures as "the burial site of last resort" for America's war dead in its early years. But a deliberate personal snub would eventually evolve into one of our nation's holiest places.

Yet beneath these solemn ranks of heroic headstones also rest many Americans whose lives were splashed by crime. Among them are victims and killers, crime-fighters and brilliant legal minds . . . good guys and bad.

Of the 184 people who died in the September 11 attack on the Pentagon, 64 are buried here in Arlington, within view of the Pentagon's west wall, where they died.

And while you might make a pilgrimage to the graves of John F. Kennedy and his brother Robert, both felled by assassins, you

Arlington National Cemetery

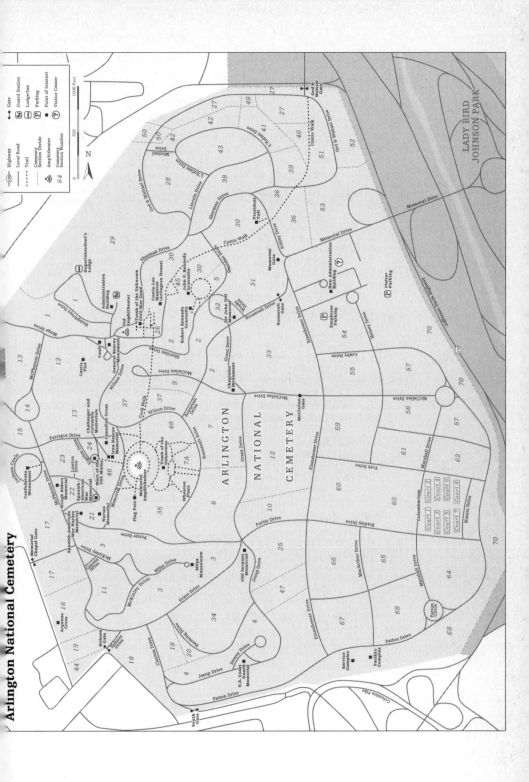

can also visit the final resting places of victims in the Fort Hood mass murder, two policemen killed by a deranged Capitol gunman, and a man who witnessed two presidential assassinations, among many others. These sites are arranged by section order, although the numbering system within the cemetery can be labyrinthine.

Arlington National Cemetery opens at 8 a.m. daily. It closes at 7 p.m. April through September, and at 5 p.m. October through March. The Visitors Center has a directory of gravesites. Admission is free. Wear comfortable shoes because visitors must walk everywhere in the 624-acre cemetery.

LOCKERBIE CAIRN
Section 1 at GPS 38.88087, -77.07488.

These 270 blocks of red Scottish sandstone—quarried near Lockerbie, Scotland—stand as a memorial to the 270 people killed when a terrorist bomb exploded Pan Am Flight 103 in midair over the Scottish village in 1988.

Just before Christmas, eleven people on the ground and 259 passengers on the plane were killed. Libyan agent Abdel Basset Ali al-Megrahi, fifty-one, was convicted and sentenced to life imprisonment in 2001 for the bombing, but he was pardoned in 2009 because he suffered from terminal prostate cancer and was supposedly on the verge of death. The controversial commutation, believed to have been tied to Libyan oil access, grew more controversial when al-Megrahi didn't actually die; he still lives comfortably in Libya.

The cairn was a gift from the Scottish people in 1993. The sandstone came from a quarry that has supplied many stones for American buildings, including the Statue of Liberty's base.

*A cairn carved from sandstone quarried near Lockerbie,
Scotland, commemorates the deaths of 270 in the 1988
terror bombing of a Pan Am jet there.*

LINCOLN'S AVENGER
Section 1, Site 690, or GPS 38.88058, -77.07720.

Lieutenant **Edward P. Doherty** (1840–1897) is credited with the capture of Lincoln assassin John Wilkes Booth at Garrett's farm in 1865. He died at age fifty-seven after a stellar career. His headstone says, COMMANDED DETACHMENT OF 16TH N.Y. CAVALRY WHICH CAPTURED PRESIDENT LINCOLN'S ASSASSIN APRIL 26, 1865.

Another soldier who played a cameo role in the assassination drama, Corporal **James Tanner** (1844–1927) is buried in Section 2, Site 877, or GPS 38.880027, -77.07352. Tanner lost both of his legs as a Union soldier and was assigned to be a clerk in Washington. The night of Lincoln's shooting, Tanner was the stenographer who recorded testimony of eyewitnesses who identified Booth. Later, he became the national commander of the Grand Army of the Republic veterans group and died at age eighty-three.

DISGRACED POLITICIAN WILLIAM BELKNAP
Section 1, Site 132, or GPS 38.88047, -77.07489.

A capable Civil War general and son of a war hero, William Worth Belknap (1829–1890) was appointed as President Grant's secretary of war in 1869. He moved to Washington and established an extravagant lifestyle, with an elegant mansion, the finest possessions, and a high-society wife who loved to throw parties for more than a thousand guests at a time. It took about seven years to discover the source of Belknap's excesses: He'd apparently been accepting bribes. He became the only Cabinet secretary ever to be impeached by the House of Representatives and resigned in disgrace (although the Senate failed to convict him on bribery charges).

His marker in Arlington suggests his affinity for lavishness. It bears a bronze relief bust of Belknap in his dress uniform on an elaborate granite base.

Although disgraced in a scandal, former Secretary of War William Belknap lies beneath an ostentatious marker.

AN OFFICER'S INSANE RAMPAGE
Section 1, Site 349, or GPS 38.88155, -77.07590.

Under the pressure of battle, even a good officer's mind can break.

On September 14, 1901, a soldier knocked on the barracks door of Captain Charles McQuiston (1858–1901), who commanded an infantry unit during the bloody Philippine Insurrection. McQuiston answered the door in a rage and drew a pistol, shooting the soldier. He then rampaged through the barracks shooting wildly until a soldier shot back and mortally wounded him.

An Army inquiry found that the West Pointer from Indiana had gone temporarily insane for reasons nobody knew. He was buried with full honors at Arlington.

THE FATHER OF AMERICAN INTELLIGENCE
Section 2, Grave 4874-A, or GPS 38.88069, -77.07068.

A genuine war hero who earned the Medal of Honor in World War I, "Wild Bill" Donovan (1883–1959) is mostly remembered today as one of America's pioneering spymasters. In 1942, he founded the US Office of Strategic Services, the sprawling wartime spyworks that would eventually become the Central Intelligence Agency. To keep his secrets secret, Donovan reported directly to his friend President Franklin D. Roosevelt and later played a behind-the-scenes role in CIA policy, especially on covert activities. Donovan was also a lawyer and was a special assistant to the chief prosecutor at the Nuremberg War Crimes in postwar Germany.

A RAGTIME MURDER VICTIM
Section 2, Site 3576, or GPS 38.87929, -77.07194.

Born in Alabama, James Europe (1881–1919) was the son of a former slave father and a free woman who encouraged their children's interest in music. As luck would have it, they moved to

Washington and lived just a few doors from composer John Philip Sousa while eight-year-old James and his sister took lessons from the Marine band's then-assistant director.

James moved to New York City in 1903, and his music career skyrocketed. He became a popular bandleader, arranger, and founder of the first black booking agency and musical union. In 1912, his Clef Club Orchestra became both the first black band and the first jazz band to play at Carnegie Hall.

In the process, Europe is credited with lifting ragtime and jazz music out of the backrooms and brothels into mainstream society.

Europe enlisted as the bandleader in the military unit that would become the famous all-black 369th Infantry Regiment. But war came and he distinguished himself as a machine-gunner, not a musician. He is said to be the first black American to lead US troops in battle during World War I. And when his regiment returned from war in 1919, Europe led his band up New York's Fifth Avenue to Harlem in a great patriotic show.

But the joy didn't last. A month later, an angry drummer stabbed Europe in the jugular with a pocketknife, killing him. He was mourned in New York City's first public funeral for a black man and buried in Arlington.

A month later, the American Legion's James Reese Europe Post #5 was founded at Washington's Navy Yard. Today, it remains an active post at 2027 North Capitol Street NE (GPS 38.917766, -77.008855).

NUREMBERG WAR CRIMES JUDGE
Section 2, Lot 4735-E, or GPS 38.88111, -77.07098.

A coal miner who became a Navy admiral and once debated the great Clarence Darrow on the topic of morality, Michael Angelo Musmanno (1897–1968) had been a Pennsylvania Supreme Court justice before he sat as a judge in the Nuremberg War Crimes trials of key Nazis after World War II in Germany. He presided over cases of the *Einsatzgruppen,* Nazi death squads that killed more than a million people.

In 1961, Musmanno also appeared as a prosecution witness at the Israeli trial of Adolf Eichmann, the architect of the Holocaust who was hanged for his crimes.

A PROMISING CAREER CUT SHORT

Section 2, Site 427-E, or GPS 38.88035, -77.07002. This grave is difficult to find by following the grave numbers; look in the northernmost corner of Section 2, just south of the intersection of Grant and Roosevelt Drives.

On July 10, 1993, Princeton honors graduate Lisa Nicole Bryant (1972–1993) had been a promising young Army officer for only a month when she was murdered during a rape attempt by a fellow soldier in her Fort Bragg dormitory. General Colin Powell, a family friend and former chairman of the Joint Chiefs of Staff, attended her funeral.

In 1994, a military jury convicted Sergeant Ervin Graves—once an honor guard in the White House—of killing Bryant with four shots from his .357-caliber Magnum. He was sentenced to life in a military prison.

A MURDEROUS CONGRESSMAN

Section 3, Site 1906, or GPS 38.87339, -77.07140.

New York Congressman Dan Sickles (1819–1914) was not just a womanizer but also a very jealous husband. When he discovered his pretty, young wife had been having an affair with his friend and US Attorney Philip Barton Key—son of "The Star-Spangled Banner" lyricist Francis Scott Key—he exploded in a rage. He ambushed Key near Lafayette Square and shot him dead. Sickles was acquitted and went on to become a Civil War general (and allegedly to have an affair with the Queen of Spain). He died at age ninety-four.

For more details, see "Congressman Kills US Attorney" in the Washington, D.C., chapter.

A MILITARY MURDER MYSTERY?
Section 3, Site 2102, or GPS 38.87279, -77.07253.

The evidence was scant: Marine 2nd Lt. James N. Sutton (1885–1907) was shot in the head beside a road to his Halligan Hall barracks (GPS 38.988191, -76.496526) on the campus of the Naval Academy in Annapolis. Although the fatal shot was fired during a scuffle with fellow officers during the wee hours after a dance at the academy, military investigators concluded Sutton committed suicide.

But Sutton's mother believed he was murdered by his brawling comrades, partly because she claimed her son's ghost told her he'd been murdered. She mounted a crusade to show that evidence had been lost or misinterpreted to cover up a murder that would embarrass the Marine Corps. Newspapers of the day, including the *New York Times*, devoted gallons of ink to the complex case as congressmen, high-ranking military officers, and a Catholic cardinal weighed in.

In 1909, Sutton's corpse was exhumed and examined closely by his mother and doctors. Certain injuries suggested he was seriously hurt in the fight and could not have shot himself, including a lack of powder burns. But a subsequent hearing failed to significantly change Sutton's manner of death, and the Marine Corps' image was preserved.

Historian Robin Cutler examined the case in her 2007 book, *A Soul on Trial: A Marine Corps Mystery at the Turn of the Twentieth*

Century. She concludes that one of Sutton's fellow officers deliberately shot him during the scuffle, and her evidence is a long history of military death cover-ups, including the friendly-fire killing of former NFL star Pat Tillman in Afghanistan.

Sutton's grave lies beneath an Oregon spruce tree believed to have been planted by his sister.

AMBUSHED BY THE KLAN
Section 3, Site 1377, or GPS 38.87441, -77.07500.

On July 11, 1964, US Army Reserve Lt. Col. Lemuel Penn (1915–1964) became an unwitting civil-rights martyr. While the decorated World War II veteran was driving through rural Georgia on his way home from active duty at Fort Benning to his home in Washington, D.C., a carload of Ku Klux Klansmen pulled alongside his Chevy Biscayne and killed him with a shotgun blast through his car window. He died instantly, eight days after the passage of the 1964 Civil Rights Act.

Two Klansmen were tried in state court for the murder but acquitted by an all-white jury. They were later convicted of federal civil-rights violations and served six years in prison. One was murdered by a friend in 1981; the other died of natural causes in 2002.

PHILANDERER ON THE FRONTIER?
Section 3, Site 2081, or GPS 38.87279, -77.07209.

A strange letter arrived on the desk of the Army's top commander in Texas in 1879. Capt. Andrew Geddes, stationed in West Texas's remote Fort Stockton, claimed that Lt. Louis Orleman was having an incestuous relationship with Orleman's eighteen-year-old daughter Lillie.

But when the accusation came to light, Orleman countercharged that it was the known womanizer Geddes who was molesting Lillie and that Geddes was only trying to muddy the case against him. In the end, the commander charged Geddes with seduction and libel.

The confusing case dragged out in the Army's longest-ever court-martial. Lillie herself testified that she had been seduced by Geddes and expected him to marry her; other witnesses claimed they'd seen Orleman make unseemly advances on his own daughter.

In the end, Geddes was convicted and sent to prison with a dishonorable discharge. But his sentence was overturned by President Rutherford B. Hayes, and Geddes went back to his troops.

In 1882, Geddes was again court-martialed for drunkenness on duty and drummed out of the Army. This time, the conviction stood, but it wasn't enough to keep him out of Arlington when he died in 1921.

A HERO TO THE END
Section 4, Lot 160, or GPS 38.87227, -77.06811.

Marion Carl (1915–1998) wasn't just one of America's most decorated air aces. The Marine pilot briefly held the world air-speed record (651 miles per hour) and world altitude record (83,235 feet), flew U-2 spy planes over Communist China, and commanded a helicopter squadron in Vietnam before retiring as a major general in 1973.

So in 1998, when a nineteen-year-old, shotgun-wielding drifter broke into Carl's Oregon home and demanded money from the general's wife, he leapt to her defense. In the ensuing scuffle, Carl's wife was wounded, but he was killed by a shotgun blast. The killer, Jesse Stuart Fanus, escaped but was later convicted, and he remains on Oregon's death row.

THE LION OF NEBRASKA
Section 4, Lot 3118-3121, or GPS 38.87201, -77.06792.

William Jennings Bryan (1860–1925) was one of the most recognized political and legal figures of his day. He ran for president three times, was elected to Congress, and served as secretary of state. But aside from being lampooned as the Cowardly Lion in L. Frank Baum's *Wonderful Wizard of Oz*, he is best known for winning one of the most celebrated criminal trials of the early 20th century: the so-called Scopes "Monkey Trial." Squaring off against superlawyer Clarence Darrow, the devout creationist Bryan helped to prosecute teacher John Scopes, accused of teaching evolution when Tennessee state law prohibited it. Bryan won the case but died five days later. His epitaph: HE KEPT THE FAITH. (Scopes's conviction was later overturned on appeal.)

See also "'Monkey Trial' Reporter's Home" (Maryland).

William Jennings Bryan helped prosecute the so-called Scopes "Monkey Trial" in 1925.

HEROIC CAPITOL POLICEMEN

Jacob Chestnut's grave is in Section 4, Site 2764-A, or GPS 38.87055, -77.06969. His fellow officer John Michael Gibson is in Section 28, Grave 140, or GPS 38.88448, -77.07165.

On July 24, 1998, US Capitol Police Special Agent John Gibson and Officer Jacob J. Chestnut—just months away from retiring— were at their posts in the Capitol when a former mental patient named Russell Eugene Weston Jr. walked through the door, put a .38-caliber handgun against Chestnut's head and fired. After also wounding a bystander, Weston went to the majority whip's office, where he was confronted by Gibson. After a furious shootout, Gibson was mortally wounded, and an injured Weston was disarmed.

The two slain policemen received the unprecedented honor of lying in state in the Capitol Rotunda, and the main eastern entrance of the Capitol (GPS 38.889803, -77.00856) was renamed the Memorial Door in their honor.

Weston later told investigators he intended to prevent the US from being eaten by hordes of diseased cannibals. He has never been charged with a crime and remains in a North Carolina mental institution.

CUCKOLDED . . . AND MURDERED?

Section 6, Site 5008-2, or GPS 38.87566, -77.07070.

The twisted mystery swirling around the death of retired Army Lt. Col. William Farber (1911–1963) is worthy of a Hollywood script.

The story starts at the end. In 1965, Dr. Carmela Coppolino was found dead by her husband, Dr. Carl Coppolino, in their new Florida home. Based on Carl's description of his wife's ongoing heart problems, her death was presumed to be a fatal heart attack, so no autopsy was done.

Less than a month later, Carl married a wealthy socialite. The story began to unravel when an agitated widow named Marjorie

Farber told police a bizarre tale. She confessed she had a fling with Carl in their New Jersey neighborhood and that they murdered her husband, William.

Two years before his wife's death, Carl gave Marjorie a syringe filled with an unknown chemical and told her to inject her husband when he slept, she said. She claimed she got cold feet, so Carl smothered her husband with a pillow while she watched. Unwittingly, Carmela Coppolino, a doctor herself, attested that Farber had died of a heart attack and signed his death certificate.

William Farber and Carmela Coppolino were exhumed. In New Jersey, Carl was charged with Farber's murder but acquitted (largely through the courtroom flamboyance of F. Lee Bailey).

However, Carmela's autopsy showed traces of succinylcholine chloride, a powerful drug that can cause muscle paralysis and heart failure. A Florida jury convicted Carl in 1967, and he served twelve years in prison before being paroled in 1979.

A HUSBAND MURDERED
Section 6, Site 9543-2 R, or GPS 38.87526, -77.07095.

Colonel Aubrey Smith (1907–1952) graduated from West Point in 1930, and his career skyrocketed. A decorated hero from World War II, he became a key commander in postwar Japan and married Dorothy Krueger, the boozy, ambitious daughter of Gen. Walter Krueger, the wartime commander of the Sixth Army. Their rocky marriage came to an explosive end the same night Smith was ordered to return to Washington. That's when Dorothy stabbed her husband with a ten-inch hunting knife, and he bled to death in their bed. He was buried here in Arlington.

Dorothy was court-martialed. A military panel convicted her and handed down a life sentence. But Dorothy's powerful father appealed on the grounds that as a civilian dependent, she should not face military justice. In 1957, the US Supreme Court eventually agreed, and

Dorothy Krueger Smith was released from prison, protected from further charges by double-jeopardy laws. The ruling forever changed how the military treated dependents accused of crimes.

(Gen. Krueger is also buried with many relatives at Arlington, in Section 30, Site 794-RH, or GPS 38.88334, -77.07070.)

INSANITY COMES HOME
Section 7, Site 8341, or GPS 38.87794, -77.07013.

Marine Col. Richard Creecy (1885–1930) had narrowly dodged death—and an odd sort of fame—at least once. In 1909, he lost a coin toss to determine who'd go up with inventor Orville Wright in an untested airplane. The plane crashed and the "winner" died, getting an airfield named for him.

By 1930, the lucky Creecy had become a high-ranking officer for the American forces stationed in Haiti. That year, he returned on leave to Washington, where he and Louise, his wife of twenty years, took a room at the Mayflower Hotel to recuperate.

For reasons still unknown, that evening Creecy attacked his wife with a small axe a little after midnight, gashing her head and fracturing her skull. While she lay bleeding, he shot himself once in the head with his service revolver. Louise died a few days later, and her husband—judged to be temporarily insane—was buried with full military honors in Arlington. Louise was buried with family in the Westminster Cemetery in Westminster, Maryland (GPS 39.569294, -76.987729).

NIXON'S ATTORNEY GENERAL
Section 7-A, Lot 121, or GPS 38.87712, -77.07110.

As President Richard Nixon's attorney general and the chairman of his reelection campaign, John N. Mitchell (1913–1988) knew many secrets. But one would prove his downfall: He paid $250,000 for the break-in and bugging of the Democratic National Committee headquarters in the Watergate Office Building at 2600 Virginia Avenue NW (GPS 38.899762, -77.05538).

For his part in the ensuing Watergate cover-up and Nixon's historic disgrace, Mitchell became the only US attorney general ever to serve prison time. He spent nineteen months in federal prison and was paroled in 1979. He died of a heart attack in 1988. As a former Navy lieutenant and Cabinet member, he was eligible for an Arlington burial.

For more about the Watergate scandal, see the entry in the Washington, D.C., chapter.

HIGH-FLYING SPY FALLS TO EARTH
Section 11, Site 685-2, or GPS 38.87320, -77.07352.

Two air crashes marked the life of Francis Gary Powers (1929–1977). The first was when his U2 spy plane was shot down over

Francis Gary Powers survived being shot down over Russia in a spy plane ... but later died in a TV helicopter crash.

Russia in 1960 and ignited one of the hottest moments of the Cold War. Reviled by American spy agencies for not destroying his plane or killing himself to avoid capture, Powers was held in a Soviet prison for two years until he was swapped for a Soviet spy in 1962.

He returned home to a cold shoulder at the CIA but worked as a test pilot and wrote a memoir, *Operation Overflight*, before he was killed in a TV news helicopter crash in Los Angeles. He was forty-seven.

AMERICA'S GREATEST MYSTERY WRITER
Section 12, Lot 508, or GPS 38.87666, -77.06868.

Although he would later become an outspoken communist, mystery writer Dashiell Hammett (1894–1961) served honorably in two world wars, earning his place in Arlington. Along the way in his famously profligate and passionate life, he wrote some of America's most enduring crime fiction (*The Maltese Falcon* and *Red Harvest*) and created a handful of memorable characters (Sam Spade and the Thin Man, among others).

See more in "Dashiell Hammett Comes of Age" (Maryland).

HE SAVED A PRESIDENT
Section 17, Lot 17719-59, or GPS 38.87654, -77.07740.

While the White House was being remodeled in the late 1940s, President Harry S. Truman moved into the nearby Blair House. On November 1, 1950, two Puerto Rican nationalists, Oscar Collazo and Griselio Torresola, stormed Blair House to assassinate Truman.

A fierce forty-second gunfight with the president's body-guards—including legendary Secret Service agent Floyd "Toad" Boring—erupted. Though mortally wounded by three bullets, Private Leslie Coffelt killed Torresola with a single shot to the head. Two other guards were wounded, but second gunman Collazo was arrested. He spent twenty-nine years in prison before being freed by President Carter in 1979, and he died in Puerto Rico in 1994 at age eighty.

Truman attended the military funeral for the former World War II infantryman Coffelt at Arlington. Torresola's body was flown home to Puerto Rico in a glass-lined steel coffin.

A plaque honoring Coffelt was erected outside the Blair House, 1651 Pennsylvania Avenue NW (GPS 38.8989, -77.038633).

"Toad" Boring died in 2008 at age ninety-two. He is buried at the Gate of Heaven Cemetery, 13801 Georgia Avenue in Silver Spring, Maryland (LOCM I, Patio K, Terrace C, #105, or GPS 39.08427, -77.06822).

ONE MAN . . . THREE ASSASSINATIONS
Section 31, Lot 13, or GPS 38.88298, -77.06967.

Few law-abiding citizens have as many bizarre connections to crime as Robert Todd Lincoln (1843–1926).

He was the oldest son of Abraham and Mary Todd Lincoln, the only one of four brothers to survive past his teens. After serving as a captain in the Union Army (where he witnessed Lee's surrender to Grant at Appomattox), he became a lawyer and, later, the secretary of war under President James Garfield.

Robert had been invited to join his parents at Ford's Theatre on April 14, 1865, but he was too tired to attend. After assassin John Wilkes Booth mortally wounded President Lincoln later that night, Robert stood at his father's bedside when he died several hours later.

On July 2, 1881, Robert was with Garfield when assassin Charles Guiteau mortally wounded the president at the Sixth Street Train Station in Washington.

And in a third tragic coincidence, Robert was attending the Pan-American Exposition in Buffalo, New York, when President William McKinley was assassinated by anarchist Leon Czolgosz on September 6, 1901, although Lincoln didn't witness the shooting.

If those twists of fate aren't eerie enough, consider this: Actor Edwin Booth once saved Robert from being crushed under a train at a New Jersey station in 1863 or 1864, before Booth's brother John assassinated Robert's father.

And Robert also owned the historic Laird-Dunlop House, a historic mansion at 3014 N Street NW (GPS 38.90667, -77.05944) that would later be occupied by *Washington Post* editor Ben Bradlee—a key figure in the Watergate scandal—and housed the backyard art studio of Mary Pinchot Meyer, victim of a high-profile 1964 murder. (Please see entries in the Washington, D.C., chapter about both.)

Robert's tomb is a short walk from Arlington's main gate and directly across the Potomac River from the Lincoln Memorial. From the intersection of Schley Drive and Custis Walk, it is about 130 yards southwest, atop the hill.

Robert Lincoln had eerie ties to three different presidential assassinations.

DEATH OF A FREEDOM FIGHTER
Section 36, Lot 1431, or GPS 38.88403, -77.06824.

After serving as a combat soldier in World War II, Medgar Evers (1925–1963) returned home with a dream of becoming a lawyer. He got his bachelor's degree and worked as an insurance salesman while volunteering for the NAACP in his native Mississippi. But when he applied to the University of Mississippi's law school in 1954, he was rejected. The NAACP made him its first Mississippi field secretary, and Evers rose to prominence as the state's most visible civil-rights activist during the height of the bloody movement.

Just after midnight on June 12, 1963, Evers was shot in the back in the driveway of his home in Jackson and died less than an hour later at a local hospital. His murder was a defining moment in the civil-rights struggle, and he was buried with full military honors at Arlington.

His killer, a segregationist named Byron de la Beckwith, was tried twice in the 1960s, but both times all-white juries failed to reach a verdict. In 1994, Beckwith was finally convicted by a mixed-race jury and sentenced to life in prison. He died in 2001 at age eighty.

FREEWAY PHANTOM VICTIM
Section 43, Site 5224-I, or GPS 38.88628, -77.06971.

On September 5, 1972, police found the strangled body of seventeen-year-old Diane Williams dumped on the shoulder of Interstate 295 just south of the District border. She'd cooked dinner for her family and then gone to her boyfriend's house before boarding a bus and vanishing. She would be the last known victim of a serial killer known as the Freeway Phantom, whose identity has never been proven conclusively. Williams was buried in Arlington as a veteran's dependent.

See more about the Freeway Phantom in the Washington, D.C., chapter.

HIGH-LIVING RUSSIAN SPY BAILS OUT
Section 43, Site 976, or GPS 38.88536, -77.07211.

In 1958, Army Sgt. Jack Dunlap (1927–1963) was a courier at the National Security Agency when Russian KGB agents promised him riches in exchange for copies of the top-secret documents he routinely carried. He gleefully accepted the offer and began living an extravagant lifestyle that soon caught the attention of his NSA bosses. In 1963, after Dunlap failed a polygraph test, he was transferred to a menial job. Fearing that he was about to be busted, he committed suicide by carbon monoxide in his car. He was buried with military honors at Arlington, and his wife later found a stash of top-secret materials in their attic.

THE KENNEDY BROTHERS
Section 45, or GPS 38.881533, -77.071467.

Two of America's most famous crime victims—John and Robert Kennedy—are buried side-by-side in one of the most somber spots at Arlington National Cemetery. And their brother, Teddy, is with them.

Assassinated by a sniper in Dallas just three days earlier, JFK was buried on November 25, 1963, his only son's third birthday. World leaders and ordinary Americans gathered at Washington's St. Matthew's Cathedral (1725 Rhode Island Avenue NW, or GPS 38.906111, -77.04) for the funeral Mass. A million dazed mourners lined the six-mile route from the Capitol to Arlington National Cemetery, where the slain president's mahogany casket was lowered into the ground, and his widow, Jacqueline, lit an eternal flame.

In 1967, JFK's remains were disinterred and moved about twenty feet to the site you see today to accommodate heavy foot traffic and build a more secure eternal flame. (Jackie was buried here, too, after she died in 1994.)

On June 5, 1968, JFK's younger brother Robert was assassinated by Sirhan B. Sirhan while campaigning for president in Los Angeles.

Assassinated President John F. Kennedy lies today with his widow, Jacqueline, under an eternal flame in Arlington.

On June 8, he was buried just to the left of John. Because his lengthy funeral train from New York was delayed, RFK's funeral is the only one ever to take place at night at Arlington National Cemetery.

In 1971, a more elaborate gravesite was designed by architect I. M. Pei for the Kennedy family, adding a granite plaza similar to JFK's and two inscriptions from RFK's most notable speeches.

In 2009, Senator Edward M. Kennedy died of a brain tumor and was buried in a sunset ceremony beside his brothers.

See more details on the JFK assassination in the Washington, D.C., chapter. See also "Mary Jo Kopechne House" (Washington, D.C.).

A MONSTER ON BASE
Section 50, Site 127, or GPS 38.88610, -77.07372.

In 1985, nineteen-year-old Marine Lance Cpl. Suzanne M. Collins was abducted while jogging at the Millington Naval Air Station outside Memphis, Tennessee. She was beaten, stabbed in the head with a screwdriver, and raped with a tree limb. Sedley Alley, a civilian, was quickly arrested and confessed to the crime. He was executed in Tennessee in 2006. Collins got a hero's burial here.

DEATH OF A SPOOK
Section 59, Lot 655, or GPS 38.87746, -77.06569.

William Colby (1920–1996) was a consummate and lifelong spy. During World War II, he volunteered for the fledgling Office of Strategic Services (OSS), where he took dangerous missions behind enemy lines. After the war, he joined the CIA, where he handled most of the intelligence gathering during the Vietnam War and directed the controversial Phoenix program. He was director of the CIA from 1973 to 1976, when he was replaced by future president George H. W. Bush.

In 1996, Colby died after suffering a heart attack while boating near his home in Rock Point, Maryland. An inquest found no signs of foul play.

RAGE IN THE RANKS
Section 59, Site 1192, or GPS 38.87770, -77.06543.

Navy Lt. (jg) Alton Grizzard had been a star quarterback for Navy. After graduation in 1991, he was assigned to the naval base in Coronado, California, where he met fellow Navy grads Ensigns Kerryn O'Neill and George Smith. While not romantically involved, Grizzard offered to walk O'Neill back to her apartment because she feared reprisals from Smith, a boyfriend she'd recently dumped.

Her fears were tragically well-founded. In December 1993, Smith showed up at the apartment and shot Grizzard four times, then shot his ex-girlfriend in the head while she cowered behind a chair. Then Smith shot himself.

O'Neill and Smith were buried in Wilkes-Barre, Pennsylvania, and Huntington Beach, California, respectively. The officer and gentleman Grizzard was laid to rest in Arlington. "I thought he was the kind of kid the whole country would read about one day, but not like this," his high school football coach said.

WRONG PLACE, WRONG TIME
Section 59, Site 9, or GPS 38.87727, -77.06596.

In 2000, Navy Lt. (jg) Scott Kinkele (1977–2000) was driving home to the Naval Air Station on Whidbey Island in Washington state from a day of hiking when he was killed by a shotgun blast through his car's rear window. A week later, three poachers were charged with Kinkele's murder, a drunken "thrill killing." Half-brothers Seth Anderson and Eben Berriault both pleaded guilty in exchange for life sentences; a third man got a lesser sentence. Anderson committed suicide in prison less than a year later.

FORT HOOD MASSACRE VICTIMS
These two graves are side-by-side in Section 59, Sites 92 and 93, or GPS 38.87868, -77.06589.

Army Lt. Col. Juanita Warman (1945–2009) wanted to serve in Afghanistan. She had been at Fort Hood in Texas for less than a day when all hell broke loose on November 5, 2009. That's when Major Nidal Hasan, a Muslim angered by the war on terror, opened fire at Fort Hood's Soldier Readiness Processing Center, killing thirteen and wounding thirty. Warman, a veteran psychiatric nurse practitioner, was the highest ranking casualty of that attack. She was fifty-five.

She was laid to rest at Arlington beside Major Libardo Caraveo, a forty-two-year-old Army psychotherapist who was also killed by Hasan. Ironically, Caraveo had led seminars on anger management, positive thinking, and diversity training.

At this writing, Hasan was awaiting a military trial for murder and could face the death penalty.

IN DEFENSE OF CHOICE
Section 60, Site 7809, or GPS 38.87536, -77.06398.

Retired Air Force Lt. Col. James H. Barrett (1919–1994) was a decorated hero who served in World War II, Korea, and Vietnam, but he didn't meet his fate on a foreign battlefield. Instead, it came on the sidewalk outside of an abortion clinic in Pensacola, Florida.

On July 29, 1994, security volunteer Barrett was escorting Dr. John Britton into the clinic when they were both shot and killed by shotgun-wielding, radical antiabortion protester Paul Hill. Barrett's wife was wounded.

Hill never denied the killings and never expressed any re-morse. In 2003, before he was executed by lethal injection in Florida, he urged abortion protesters to "do what you have to do to stop [abortion]."

A KILLER HUNTS POLICE
Section 60, Site 7834, or GPS 38.87570, -77.06397.

Veteran homicide detective and former Marine Henry J. Daly (1943–1994) was killed when an angry murder suspect opened fire with an assault weapon in the Metropolitan Police Department's cold-case office. Two FBI agents also died, and two other people were wounded before the gunman killed himself.

The Metropolitan Police Department headquarters (300 Indiana Avenue NW, or GPS 38.8945, -77.016561) were later renamed the Henry J. Daly Building in honor of the twenty-eight-year veteran.

A REAL-LIFE SPY THRILLER
Section 63, Columbarium Court 3, Section LL, Stack 14, Niche 5, or GPS 38.87517, -77.06143.

Fred Woodruff (1947–1993) was a CIA agent assigned to the American embassy in the former Soviet republic of Georgia. On August 8, 1993, he was shot in the head in his Russian-style Jeep just a few days before he was to return to the US. A teenage soldier confessed to the shooting and claimed it was accidental, but two years later, Georgian intelligence agents claimed Woodruff had been killed by the Russian KGB. The soldier who had been jailed for the murder was released, but Woodruff's killers have never been identified.

The marble plaque on Woodruff's columbarium vault identifies him only as an ordinary Army specialist, 5th class.

A KILLER'S FORMER GRAVE
Section 63, Columbarium Court 5, Section PP, Stack 27, Niche 6, or GPS 38.87513, -77.06084.

Life took some wrong turns for Vietnam veteran Russell Wayne Wagner (1952–2005), but few as sharp as his death. Wagner was convicted in 2002 for the stabbing murders of an elderly Hagerstown, Maryland, couple and sentenced to life in prison. After he died of a heroin overdose in 2005, his body was cremated, and his sister asked that his ashes be interred at this columbarium in Arlington National Cemetery.

The victims' family was outraged. They asked that Wagner's ashes be removed from Arlington's hallowed spaces and that new laws prohibit killers from ever being buried there.

In 2006, Congress passed a law forbidding anyone convicted of a capital crime from burial in a national cemetery. In 2007, Wagner's ashes were returned to his family.

9/11'S VICTIMS
Section 64, or GPS 38.87345, -77.06092.

Three-year-old Dana Falkenberg was headed with her older sister and parents on a dream vacation to Australia when they boarded American Airlines Flight 77 at Dulles International Airport on September 11, 2001.

But before the morning was over, Dana and her family had perished when their plane slammed into the west wall of the Pentagon, killing 125 people in the building and all sixty-four aboard the plane. All but five of the victims were identified.

Among the unknown remains in the Pentagon rubble was little Dana. Their cremated ashes were placed in a single casket and buried within view of the Pentagon beneath a five-sided granite marker bearing the 184 names. The unidentified remains were retired Army colonel Ronald Golinski, sailor Ronald Henanway, Army employee Rhonda Rasmussen, Navy employee James T. Lynch, and Dana Falkenberg.

For more details about the attack, please see the entry for the 9/11 Pentagon Memorial in the Washington, D.C., chapter.

The ashes of five unidentified victims of the Pentagon's 9/11 terror attack lie under this monument in Arlington National Cemetery.

ACKNOWLEDGMENTS

This is my third book in the Crime Buff's Guide series and, like its predecessors, it didn't just appear under my pillow like a gift from some demented fairy. It required a kind of passionate, unofficial, and unpaid support staff to point the way to the places I've described. I was blessed.

And, once again, my chief blessing is my devoted wife, Mary, who has ridden shotgun on most of my ghost-chasing explorations. She has developed a keen eye, a navigator's grace under pressure, and a patient spirit. And her presence reminds me repeatedly that when a man drags his wife to dozens of muddy cemeteries, old crime scenes, and presumably haunted buildings, and she tells him she wouldn't want to be anywhere else, then he knows he chose the right one.

Many others helped, too, by being there when I called. I must extend my warmest thanks to Corinne May Botz; Robert C. Capel; Barry Cauchon and John Elliott; Roman Coale; Jimmy Coates; Cindy Collins; George Denny; Michael Dobbs; Tim "Cosgrove" Jones; Sue Khalil; Richard Layman; James Lesar; Terri Maxfield; Amy McGovern; John Michael; Michael Robert Patterson; Jack and Marnie Sarver; Vic Socotra; Bob Teates; James Trainum; Ruth Trocolli; Karen Valentine; Leslie Walker; and Dr. Robert Watson of Lynn University.

... and to all the rest who happily led me through their homes, scribbled directions, said "follow me," called other people "who should know," and shared memories that nobody ever asks about anymore.

—Ron Franscell

INDEX

ABOUT THE AUTHOR

Ron Franscell is a bestselling author and journalist whose atmospheric true crime/memoir *The Darkest Night* was hailed as a direct descendant of Truman Capote's *In Cold Blood* and established him as one of the most provocative new voices in narrative nonfiction. His lyrical and evocative road-memoir, *The Sourtoe Cocktail Club* (Globe Pequot Press), won critical acclaim across North America. *The Crime Buff's Guide to Outlaw Washington, DC* is the third in his crime/history/travel series. Ron grew up in Wyoming and now lives in Texas.

PHOTO BY MARY FRANSCELL